UNLEASH YOUR SUPERNOVA

UNLEASH YOUR SUPERNOVA

101 ACTION STEPS TO BOOST CREATIVITY AND BEAT BURNOUT!

NOVA LORRAINE

AWARD-WINNING FOUNDER OF *RAINE MAGAZINE*

Skyhorse Publishing

Skyhorse Publishing books may be purchased in bulk at special discounts for sales promotion, corporate gifts, fund-raising, or educational purposes. Special editions can also be created to specifications. For details, contact the Special Sales Department, Skyhorse Publishing, 307 West 36th Street, 11th Floor, New York, NY 10018 or info@skyhorsepublishing.com.

Visit our website at www.skyhorsepublishing.com.

10 9 8 7 6 5 4 3 2 1

Library of Congress Cataloging-in-Publication Data is available on file.

Jacket design by Daniel Brount
Jacket illustration by Shutterstock
Author photo by Vital Agibalow

Print ISBN: 978-1-5107-6332-6
Ebook ISBN: 978-1-5107-6333-3

Printed in the United States of America

I dedicate this book to my mom and dad, as well as my dear husband and children for inspiring me to go after my dreams.

I am also truly grateful for the family and friends that supported me along my roller-coaster ride of entrepreneurship.

CONTENTS

FOREWORD

As an entrepreneur, innovator, business transformation consultant, professor of entrepreneurship and innovation, and director of a university-based research center dedicated to understanding and supporting new venture creation, I have encountered countless entrepreneurs who have effectively addressed customer pain points, exploited unique market opportunities, and bridged gaps between what is and what could be, but none have so courageously lifted the curtain on the inner workings of the mind and heart in these endeavors as Nova Lorraine in this book. Most academics and students of business view entrepreneurship as a somewhat mechanical, step-by-step process involving ideation, product development, business planning, prototyping, and startup launch. Much less attention has been focused, however, on the person, the soul of the entrepreneur over time, and the evolution of core values and beliefs that are the underpinnings of innovation. I was struck by the revelatory notion of Nova's book which posits that the process of turning inward, becoming authentically introspective, is essential to discovering and unleashing one's hidden entrepreneurial potential. In sum, introspection is key to having and fulfilling dreams, whether in business or any other context.

According to Nova, the journey to becoming an entrepreneur is a deeply personal, transformative experience involving confronting, discovering, and ultimately accepting one's power of agency to choose a destiny. The destiny one chooses may, if desired, become explosively creative, even profitable, from a business standpoint, but only after digging down into the hidden layers of the soul to honestly examine and question oneself. Knowing your "whys," says Nova, is a foundational entrepreneurial pillar. Having uncovered the whys of your life, not the superficial whys, but the real whys and motives of your life that are intimately tied to heart and passion, you expose the bedrock upon which to build and create. It is upon this bedrock that volcanos of passion and positive energy flourish. An often neglected topic in the world of entrepreneurship is the unfolding pathway of the self that leads to discovering purpose, finding a path forward into creation, and tapping into the reasons behind the desires and the dreams that can eventually become business realities.

I love the way Nova so eloquently spins straw, represented by a world of uncertainty, surprises, barriers, and unforeseen adversity, into a golden fleece of personal growth and future success. Here again, it is her uncanny and unique ability to teach us how to build on challenges, barriers, even mundane experiences of life, to fuel our own supernovas. Her advice is practical, accessible, positive, and forever optimistic and forward-thinking. The reader will find oceans of wisdom embedded in many straightforward tips like: keep alert and be ready to notice the little things, give and be ready to receive, keep track of your ideas, admit you are creative, and acknowledge your brilliance. Deriving wisdom from elemental ideas and daily experience is Nova's talent. How better to communicate the enduring lessons of life and precursors to unleashing one's supernova than to reveal what a paper route can teach you?

Reading this book made me wish I had journaled more, reflected more, pondered the course of my life with more intent, become more mindful of the lessons embedded in adversity, and been as attentive to the undulating fabric of life as Nova. Likewise, I wish I had derived as much wisdom from my own journey, as I sought out successes in business, research, and teaching. What clearly comes across from reading this book is how much one can learn by being mindful with the intent to improve one's life and surroundings. Being mindful of habits, opportunities to give and receive, what you are known for, sources of joy, emerging visions and dreams, and when the time is right to act are all ingredients to personal growth.

One of the most profound takeaways from Nova's writing is the idea that launching a business venture is closely paralleled by personal growth, through increased awareness, and self-creation. It dawns on me that the entrepreneur isn't just engaging in the monetization of an idea, such as a new product or business model, but is also dedicated to unleashing one's own potential. The higher-order theme of this book is encapsulated in a quote from Steven Pressfield's *The War of Art*: "Our job in this life is not to shape ourselves into some ideal we imagine we ought to be, but to find out who we already are and become it."

There is perhaps nothing more difficult than to be critically aware of oneself and the assumptions and presuppositions of one's thoughts. What could be more valuable to creativity and entrepreneurship than becoming conscious of one's own consciousness and potential? I believe that is, ultimately, what Nova is trying to teach us. Human beings are capable of scrutinizing and evaluating their own thoughts, emotions, values, and assumptions in order to unleash something greater. Once identified and exposed to the light, the hidden strengths of a person are subject to the forces of individual agency. In other words, our desire to grow, change, and make a difference. Rooting out old or embedded assumptions is definitely a starting point to unleashing our individual supernovas.

The idea that we discover and unleash new realities by framing and labeling experiences in positive ways is a major underlying theme of this book. The language we use to label experiences, including the attitudes we bring to the ups and downs of our journey, is one of the keys to bridging the gap between creativity and entrepreneurship. Over time, we begin to believe that from different words come different realities, just as we can take negative experiences and reframe them as opportunities. Such a mindset is an effective way to derive lessons for future benefit. For example, in Nova's words, you can take what bugs you and other people, keep a list of them, and eventually, over time, translate them into opportunities for business. In her eyes, everything is an opportunity to learn, grow, improve, and dream.

There is much to be said of building bridges and spanning boundaries in this book. The fuel for an entrepreneur's supernova is moving beyond comfort zones, looking outside one's industry for inspiration, reading the biographies of creative people, connecting unique and disparate data points through mind mapping, and listening to employees to find ideas that lead to breakthroughs. Connectivity between people, ideas, memories, the past, present, and future is an engine of the starburst of ideas and creativity needed for entrepreneurship. There is so much to be said of the heart and soul of the entrepreneur and how supernovas are unleashed from the inside out. Better to leave the details of this process to the reader of this marvelous book.

—Dr. Shawn M. Clark, director of the Farrell Center for Corporate Innovation and Entrepreneurship (FCFE)

PREFACE

A friend of mine recently asked me how I went about getting a book published. I stated matter-of-factly, "It's been in the making for years and the stars magically aligned a few months ago." As the words came out of my mouth, I knew I needed to elaborate further as I didn't want to underestimate the preparation, research, time, determination, teamwork, and "stick to it" mindset that was needed for it all to come together, especially during a pandemic. I realized at that moment that I was describing what it took and often takes for a creative to bring an idea to life.

This book was always inside of me. Truthfully, my life is the backdrop to the words on each page. As I experienced one life-altering moment after another, and then chose to share it with a friend or stranger that cared to listen, I would often hear, "You should write that down. Your story is so inspiring and it can really help people." Those words were repeated over and over again until one day, I took them to heart and had the aha moment I needed to commit to what seemed an elusive feat. I knew deep down that instead of casually sharing my stories for entertainment, to sometimes just make myself chuckle (even with the tales that ended so badly), I could collect them in a way that could shed light on an incredible journey of creative entrepreneurship. I could help others navigate the roller-coaster ride we call life, as we embark on a pursuit of happiness through the efforts of turning our passions into profit.

I felt that although many books exist about entrepreneurship, not many described the good, the bad, and the ugly of our unpredictable daily reality. Even worse, fewer talked about the tools needed for a designer, writer, photographer, techy, architect, or artist to navigate the journey of staying creative and not burning out on this marathon of entrepreneurship. I hope my joys and pains along with the wisdom I have discovered along the way help you or someone you love find happiness while empowering you to never give up on your dreams.

CHAPTER ONE

On cloudy days, be patient for that glorious moment when the sky parts way for a beautiful beam of light that warms everything in its path.

~

YOU AND ONLY YOU DECIDE YOUR FUTURE

I felt a pit in my stomach when I heard those words. For some reason, hearing them felt worse than reading them on the six-foot projector screen at the front of the lecture hall. It was only a couple of weeks into my freshman year in college when the professor shared with the rest of the three hundred or more students in Sociology 101 that I, based on my demographic profile, belonged to the group that sat at the last rung of the ladder in society. Yes, I, Nova, had the most obstacles that lay in front of me in accomplishing "success" according to our sociological system.

Well, the professor didn't actually call out my name, but his words carried through the air like a boulder in the wind of a tornado. As I looked around the class and saw that I was the lone representative for the group he was describing, the pit in my belly grew bigger. As the confusion, embarrassment, and anger built inside me, something even more powerful was building too. I felt a fuel like no other to prove him, history, and the "system" wrong.

"Just tell me that I can't do something and see what happens." This was my motto that worked well for me throughout school and beyond. However, launching a business as a young mother, this intention was not as simple a task as I thought it would be. Sometimes persistence and passion are not the only tools you need in your tool belt to accomplish your dreams. Join me on a roller-coaster journey of discovering tips, hacks, and words of wisdom to help thrive on the path of creative entrepreneurship.

We are all born into a family. Coming into the world as infants, our family environment is determined by someone else. However, as we grow into adults, what we do in life is all up to us. It is important for each of us to remember that when it comes to our actions, we always have a choice. Many of us mistakenly believe that our beginnings in life predestine the path we take and the decisions we make from then on. We seem to forget that we are the writers of our story, the creators of our world, the directors in our own play. We tend to hand over the power we hold to everything or everyone outside of us. For example, we let data or statistics be the reason we select one path or another, or we allow hurtful words to hold us back. How often has a traumatic memory been the wall between us and our dreams? I speak from the heart because I have experienced all of these things firsthand. I had many, many opportunities throughout my life to stop trying. However, I found the insight, strength, and perseverance to always push forward no matter what, with one goal in mind: to never give up on my dreams. No matter the struggle, or what the data or statistics may say, you can always choose what you want out of life, so never let the numbers lie to you. Instead, dig deep, and let your dreams guide you.

> "Others have seen what is and asked why. I have seen what could be and asked why not."
> —Pablo Picasso

IT STARTS WITH THE "WHY"

One day, a colleague and friend, Ryon Anderson, mindset coach and brain theory expert, asked me a simple question: "Why?"

"Why?" I repeated back to him.

"Yes. Why are you are doing what you are doing? I want you to really think about that. I want you to go back to your original 'Why,'" he said.

I paused for a long moment as I thought to myself: *Why*? It's been a long time since I thought about this, and this was the first time I was asked to go back to my original inspiration behind all that I was doing. Quite a few years had passed since the day I chose this unpredictable path that I am currently on. After a moment of silence, I took a mental trip back to my past to the time when I was not yet married, a mother, or a seasoned creative. I hadn't any entrepreneurial endeavors of my own or even lived in a big city. During that phase in my life, although very young and naive, I was full of passion and had a clear vision for what I wanted to do in life, and more importantly, why. Then, my thoughts jolted me back to the present moment. I pondered, *What about now*?

After my coach's question sunk in, I realized that of course I knew the answer. *To help people*, I thought to myself. It's always been about aiding others. For as long as I can remember, since high school when I made the decision to become a doctor, I have always wanted to make others happy, especially kids. At that young age, I believed the only way to do this was through the most obvious path: medicine. Psychiatric medicine, to be more exact. As years passed, the why didn't change but the *how* did.

It is okay if your method of getting to your end goal changes, as long as the reason you are doing it still feels right. You want your why to bring more joy into your life than you can ever imagine, not just fill your days with a never-ending task list. If your why isn't in tune with your purpose, eventually your plan will break down and your once clear path will slowly start to disappear. All of a sudden, without warning, you will seem unfulfilled without understanding the cause. This is when the why question usually shows itself. However, you don't have to wait to get to this point. Start first with asking yourself "why," and making sure that the response is authentically you at the present moment.

Remember, you don't want to charge ahead because it will make your friends or family happy. It should always be because it makes you actualize a greater version of yourself. Your why should not only bring you joy when thinking about it, it should be an integral part of your personal growth. Without growth, we stagnate, get bored, depressed, or aggressive. These emotions are all cues for when we need to do a why check-in with any or all aspects of our life.

KNOW YOUR "WHY"

Grab a pen and paper for an exercise that can change everything for you and give you clarity about where you are right now versus where you want to be. This exercise is going to help you flush out the true *why* behind your most burning goal in this current moment. I call it the "why check." Redo this exercise every three months to see if you are still on track for your most desired wants in life.

It's important to check in with yourself often to make sure that the energy you are putting into your job, tasks, or projects is always helping to support your why. It can be easy to get off track and lose yourself in the hamster wheel of circumstance. Asking yourself the following questions can help you get to the real root of the reasons behind your wants and clarify if the desires you seek will bring growth and happiness or just more work and possibly misery over time. Use the following example as a guide.

1. Ask yourself, "Why am I doing XYZ task?"
   Q: Why am I studying nursing?
   A: My parents expect me to become a nurse.

2. Take that response and ask the question again.
   Q: Why?
   A: They believe nursing will allow me to financially support myself.

3. Take the last answer and apply the "why" question to that too.
   Q: Why?
   A: They believe nursing is the only guarantee for me to become financially stable.

In total, you will have asked yourself why three times. By the third response, bells should be dinging, and ears should be ringing with a lot of aha moments. Look at your third response and pay attention to how that response makes you feel. If you feel happy or positive, push forward, full speed ahead. If you feel anger, frustration, hesitation, or any other negative feeling, take a moment to consider if your reasons for doing the task sit well with you. If they don't, slow down a bit to give yourself time to reflect and adjust your course.

Now that you have figured out your "why" to a certain action or goal, how does it fit into your purpose? If you have not yet defined what your purpose is, how does the response to the third why question make you feel?

1. Good
2. Not so good

Another way of approaching this is to ask yourself:

1. Do you *like* your answer to the third why question?
2. Do you *love* it?

The goal in life is to get closer to what you love—always. What do you do if you answer "not so good" or "like" to the above queries? It's time to reevaluate what you are doing and make steps to change course. In other words, abort ship. The faster you can avoid wasting time on anything that pulls you away from your love, purpose, or want list, the better. Yes, I said wasting. It may sound harsh, but it is the truth. Time is precious; it is the most valuable resource you have. You cannot create it, buy it, or get it back. If you look at it that way, always, you will think carefully over everything you choose to do. With so many choices in life, why spend a moment on actions that lead you nowhere?

DISCOVERING MY "WHY"

Growing up in a Caribbean immigrant household, I thought becoming a doctor was the only way I could answer my desire to help others. Out of six siblings, I am fourth in line and the last to be born in Jamaica before my parents became residents of the United States. The pressure was on to pick a career that would guarantee me a successful financial future and also be considered respectable and/or prestigious in the eyes of my parents who came to the US to seek more opportunities for their family.

I looked to my older brothers for inspiration and quickly zeroed in on the one that was three years older because, as young kids, he really enjoyed helping me with my homework and made school a priority. For as long as I could remember, I looked up to him and admired him for his love of learning and his focus on education. When he made his declaration to become a doctor, I couldn't wait to follow in his footsteps. My parents highly approved of this career path for me and were excited to support me along the way. My siblings and I were the first generation to go to college in this country.

They say time flies but who actually believes that until they become parents and their days and years are marked by their children's achievements and graduations? Who knew that my adult years would be the start of the continuation of what my parents started? I soon birthed children that became the second generation in my immediate family to go to college. I also made some life-changing decisions that took me off the path of medicine and on the roadway to fashion and entrepreneurship.

I wrote this book for the many individuals pivoting in their careers as I once did, as well as the many students with aspirations that I once had. This resource comes from a unique point of view. I am an immigrant born to a family that came to this country with nothing but their dreams. I am a daughter who watched her parents start a business without a network or investors. I am a woman who launched her fashion company with a $500 business loan with a one-year-old and another on the way. I have shared some of my life experiences in these pages to give an extra nudge of hope for those on the fence of doubt or change. My ultimate goal is to inspire you to never give up on your goals.

> "Creativity takes courage."
> —Henri Matisse

A NEW GENERATION OF TRAILBLAZERS

"Mom, I want to be an entrepreneur." When I heard these words first from my oldest teenage son, and soon after from his younger sister, I wasn't sure how I felt. It was not entirely surprising, for this has been the journey they witnessed their mother experience their entire lives. However, if they chose to follow my path, I also knew the challenges that lie ahead for the both of them. As I dug a little deeper, I noticed more and more of their generation having the same desires. Fifty-four percent of millennials are choosing to pursue starting their own venture—a true adventure in the unknown. This does not take into account the increasing percentage of mid-lifers pivoting from their long-standing careers to do the same. Looking for books to refer them to for guidance, I noticed a lack of resources that discussed how to successfully survive the marathon of entrepreneurship, especially for creative entrepreneurs.

The need to increase awareness regarding the tools necessary to balance creativity, overcome burnout, and endure the roller-coaster ride of entrepreneurship is what propelled me to write this book. You will learn more about finding the brilliance within yourself and your ideas, the less glamorous side of creative entrepreneurship, the connection between mindfulness and productivity, and how to ultimately go from idea to execution in all that you do. This book is the ultimate guide for anyone using their gifts and talents to build into their livelihoods. It is a resource accompanied by anecdotes, personal stories, and inspiring W.O.Ws (words of wisdom). I wrote this book to share my mistakes and successes as well as insight from some of the top talents in the world to show you that you can achieve anything you set your mind to.

W.O.W

"It's okay to dream. You're worth it."

CHAPTER TWO

We often live too far into the future or stuck somewhere in the past. It is only and always the present moment that matters.

~

PLANNING FOR THE UNEXPECTED

Wow! I did it! I thought to myself after hanging up the phone. I couldn't contain my emotions any longer; I suddenly belted out a scream of laughter and leaped into the air—heels and all. "I got the job!" Not bad after just a couple weeks of searching. *Who knows where this will take me*, I thought. Getting a job offer at an IT recruiting firm was certainly unexpected but also the start of a new adventure.

After spending a short while finding and moving into my new apartment, I was now going to do what most people do after college: learn how to live like an adult. It's funny looking back and thinking how anxious I was to graduate college and start working a "real" job. Growing up, we fantasize about being an adult, living on our own, making our own money and, the best part, spending it however we like. The reality is, if you are not doing what you love, there is nothing fun about adulting, especially if you are making money doing mostly what you don't like and spending it primarily on bills. So . . . if you are going to work anyway, choose your work environment carefully. If only half of your work day is occupied with activities you like, your work environment will add to your personal growth.

Backing up three weeks, my summer was going to be very different. In other words, going right into the workforce after graduating college wasn't the original plan. Instead, I was well on my way to moving to Washington, D.C., to start a PhD program in clinical psychology. Before I was able to schedule the moving van southbound, the unexpected happened. On my last night as an official undergraduate, my boyfriend invited me out to dinner to celebrate this huge milestone in my life. Unbeknownst to me, he planned a beautiful dinner for the two of us in which he asked the life-changing question: "Will you marry me?" I, of course, said yes!

Now newly engaged, I decided not to move out of Connecticut, and instead take a year off from grad school to plan my wedding and reapply to doctoral programs closer to my soon-to-be husband. For some, putting their educational dreams on hold would have been nonnegotiable. For me, it was a chance to choose a new adventure while keeping my priorities in mind. Knowing that I would still go on to grad school, even if it was pushed out a bit in the future, staying in the same state with my fiancé to prepare for a life together took the lead. Most importantly, I made the choice without regrets or hesitation. When faced with unexpected forks in the road throughout life, all roads can bring you closer to happiness, if you intentionally plan for that outcome.

TIPS FOR PLANNING FOR THE UNEXPECTED

1. **Stay open-minded**: If you feel that a recent announcement or event is going to throw you way off track, take a pause and reflect on the good that can come from this. Know that there is always a positive side to any situation. We've seen in history that one person's tragedy can create lessons or insights to protect a great number of people or things from future suffering.

2. **Play the "what is the worst thing" game**: When you are unsure about something you had your heart set on, ask yourself what the worst thing would be if this never came to pass. Sometimes, just visualizing yourself living through that experience is enough to show you that the worst imagined situation really isn't so bad. Visualization is a powerful tool. It tricks our brains into going through a physical event without it taking place but still allows us to resolve the negative emotions that could come with the experience if it happened in real life.

3. **Learn to let go and make room for something greater**: If you are okay with losing anything you have put a lot of value into, nothing will ever be able to really knock you down for good. If an item you really wanted never comes or something you cherish gets taken away from you, know that it is making way for something better. Think of life as a roller-coaster. The roller-coaster never ends at the lowest point. The lowest point is actually the signal that the worst is over.

4. **Just breathe**: Most of us walk around the majority of the time taking short, shallow breaths, limiting the oxygen going to the crucial points within our body and allowing unexpected events to more easily jar us. However, if we focus on

taking deeper breaths more often, we can pave the way for a stronger foundation to withstand any moment. Deeper breaths place our bodies in a calmer state, creating a buffer for sudden experiences that may be perceived negatively.

5. **Learn the "any outcome" mantra**: This mantra states that any outcome is a good outcome. Just imagine walking around repeating this to yourself all day, every day. Think of all the times you were late, failed a test, got injured, etc. If you believed that someday you would see positive results from those negative experiences, nothing would ever rattle you again. If you were fired from a job, for example, perhaps that was your way of getting a ticket to freedom or on the path to your dream life, home, or partner.

> "Creativity requires the courage to let go of certainties."
> —Erich Fromm

WHEN "I QUIT" SAVED MY LIFE

It was a typical day of work. I woke up around 7:00 a.m. to get showered and dressed. I would build in just enough time to stop at the coffee shop across the street from work to get my usual café latte, hazelnut flavored, with a warm baked chocolate chip cookie. Coffee was the only thing that successfully got me through the monotony of working in a lonely gray office with two other people, my boss who was a little neurotic, and my coworker, a cool recent college grad like myself who mourned the party life he left behind.

My coworker came in late every day and did half the work I did and was rewarded a company cruise with my boss. What did I get for my efforts of being the new whiz kid hire that was breaking all prior office sales records? I was granted the promise of quickly rising in the field of IT recruiting, but nothing was moving fast enough. The nine-to-five days seemed to drag from eight hours to twelve hours although I knew this was impossible. It just felt longer, even though I arrived and left at the same time each day.

The day finally arrived that would thrust me on a trajectory of no return. My coworker strolled in at 9:20 a.m., tie in hand. He started his usual spiel about how much he missed his college fraternity brothers, and then about how excited he was for his new company car. I slowly asked, "You're getting a company car?"

"Yup," he said. "I even picked out the color. Dark blue," he proudly bragged. It took everything in me not to scream: "For what? You come in late every day, only work half of the time, and don't have close to my sales records!" Instead, I gave him a gentle smile and walked slowly back to my office. I forced myself to hold back my tears over the grossly obvious mistreatment I felt.

It took everything in me to get through the rest of the day. When 5:00 p.m. hit, I quickly gathered my things and headed to the car. I couldn't get home fast enough. When I finally arrived, I opened the door, ran to my bedroom, and threw myself onto my mattress, burying my face into my pillow. Then, I screamed! I let out everything held back at the office and let the tears stream down my face. In that moment, I asked myself, *If you could do anything, anything at all, without worrying what someone would think or say, what would it be?* Fashion design immediately popped into my head. That was the first day of the last day of being treated unfairly at any job. (Well, almost . . . more about that later.)

Getting back to my new revelation regarding fashion, just the thought of it brought me instant peace. The tears stopped almost immediately, and I began pondering this whacky idea even more. I started thinking of all the reasons why I shouldn't take this thought seriously. I hadn't taken a drawing class since middle school, and that was architectural drafting. Although I loved it, did that even count? Not to mention, what would my parents think, my fiancé who had just finished medical school, and my new in-laws to be? Would they all wonder if I was going crazy? I didn't grow up around fashion or art, just a very stylish mom and a set of aunts who had killer sewing skills and a knack for looking amazing from head to toe every time they stepped out the door. Instead of an artistic background, I was armed with a bachelor's degree in science and would be giving up a childhood dream of becoming a doctor in order to become a fashion designer. It all seemed like such a stretch. As soon as that brief moment of joy came, a feeling of frustration followed, as I asked myself why I was choosing to go after such an unrealistic dream.

I am a person that has always planned things. Predictability as well as assurance of the next step was part of what brought me comfort in my experiences. However, something shifted inside of me. My mind started to ponder the routine of the silver, three-level building that had become my home for eight hours a day over the past few months. What became a security blanket, the concept of routine and predictable outcomes, now seemed more like wearing a heavy weighted vest. My routine was simple and consistent, yet uninspiring.

As I visualized my daily routine, the option of choosing fashion as a new career path, although the most uncertain and unpredictable thing that I would have done to date, uncertainty and unpredictability felt more fulfilling than anything I was currently doing. I knew the choice I had to make. There was no way I could continue down what seemed an increasingly dreadful road. I had to do something very out of character . . . I needed to quit a job that offered not only security but, in time, great financial reward.

SIGNS FOR KNOWING WHEN TO QUIT

Are you currently in a school major, job, or role on your team that you have second thoughts about? Most of us are taught to see something through to the end, to stick it out no matter what. Quitters are losers, right? Quitters can actually be the winners when they recognize when to let go of the things in their life that are not allowing them to grow but instead creating a downward spiral of misery. To help clarify when you should consider quitting as a solution, ask yourself the following questions:

1. Do you wake up feeling anxious or stressed in the morning before starting your day?
2. Do you make little effort in selecting what to wear or preparing for your day?
3. Do you avoid speaking or smiling to those around you on your way to your school or place of work when the opportunity arises?
4. Do you find yourself turning to food to cheer you up throughout the day?
5. Are you short tempered with those closest to you?
6. Do you feel a sigh of relief or an immediate lift in your mood when your workday or school day is over?
7. Are you feeling less than enthusiastic more than half of the day?

If you answered yes to three or more of these questions, it is time to reevaluate what you are currently doing. As a mother, quitting is the last thing I want my child to do, but what I have learned throughout my life and raising four children is that happiness is the real key to success. Pounding the pavement and putting daily time into a negative environment is different than pushing through a challenging situation or overcoming an insurmountable obstacle to reach your goals. If a role, job, or academic major is only going to continue to decrease your state of mind or perpetuate negative outcomes and thoughts about yourself and others, it's time to choose you and say, "I quit!"

W.O.W

No job is worth your misery.

CHAPTER THREE

Your true light will always shine to others,
if you allow them to see you for who you really are.

~

ADVICE THAT CHANGED EVERYTHING

The accountant at the company I first worked for had become a dear friend. When I told her my plans for leaving the organization and what I wanted to pursue next, she gave me a valuable piece of advice. I will never forget that morning. We were riding up in the elevator heading to start our day at the office when I tentatively shared this unexpected news with her. Once I got it all out, she was overjoyed with my decision to follow my heart and said, "No matter what you do moving forward, remember one thing: tell everyone you meet what you want to do. You will be surprised how many people will want to help you."

After an afternoon of confusion and tears as I questioned what I wanted to do with my life, I decided to leave my job and pursue uncharted territory in the world of art and fashion. It started with a few long conversations with those closest to me: my fiancé, my parents, and finally my in-laws. I wondered before every conversation who would be supportive and less encouraging. Surprisingly, neither set of parents nor my fiancé tried to talk me out of this crazy notion of becoming a fashion designer. They were all very excited about this new chapter in my life. Perhaps my own enthusiasm helped in convincing them. Next on my agenda . . . hit the books, the Internet, and talk to anyone who would listen. I was determined to learn as much as I could about this mysterious field of fashion that I knew nothing about.

Going back to my friend, the accountant, she later gave me the contact information to a friend, a designer who worked for Macy's in New York City and said, "Call him. Tell him I referred you to him and what you want to do, and he will take it from there." I thankfully accepted the note and gave her a hug. The circumstances that followed after I met him changed my life.

I only remembered New York City from a couple of visits when I was really young and what I heard or saw on TV. My impression of Manhattan was a place that was dirty, unsafe, and unfriendly. Despite this naive concept of the Big Apple, I got up my courage and took the three-hour bus ride from Hartford, Connecticut, to meet Angela's friend in New York. The meeting was well worth the anticipation and the long, not-so-pleasant bus trip. He was the first bona fide fashion professional I had ever met, and over lunch he opened up about the world of possibilities that existed in the industry. I was intrigued more than ever. He then suggested I take another trip to New York to meet a friend of his, a talented fashion designer from Parsons, one of the most prestigious design schools in the world! This friend later give me advice that would change my reality. What she so graciously shared was the knowledge that helped me put together a fashion portfolio, the one thing that almost prevented me from applying to design school in the first place.

LEARN TO RECOGNIZE YOUR MESSENGERS

Do you remember old movies with the messenger pigeons or the talking ravens or even the dove in the story of Noah's Ark? These tales show us over and over again how birds can deliver timely messages with information that often can save our life. Well, people can do the same thing if we take advantage of the times when these messengers come into our life. Have you ever met someone you felt an immediate connection with, someone who you trusted right away with your secrets or inner thoughts? Have you ever found yourself in a situation where timing seemed too perfect, you were led to a stranger who offered help, or bumped into an old friend? Well, the universe is always conspiring in our favor, if we pay attention to receive the goodies offered to us. Below are five ways to find your messengers and receive the information that will lead you closer to your dreams.

1. **When out and about, keep alert and be ready to notice the little things around and the strangers to say hello to**: This may be hard at times as we are often distracted with our mobile devices. Trust me, if you sacrifice a little time away from emails and social media to stay focused on your surrounding environment, you will find the breadcrumbs you are looking for.

2. **Go out of your way to speak to someone that brings a sense of comfort, warmth, or trust**: Offer them a compliment, say a greeting, or ask them a question. You may be surprised by where that simple gesture can lead you and what knowledge could come from the conversation started.

3. **Have your top want for the day, week, or year to stay top of mind and ready to share with whomever will listen**: As humans, we genuinely want to help others. We love sharing

our knowledge and helping another person along their journey. When you meet the right person that triggers the warm fuzzies, share your biggest want with them, and get excited for what's to come.

4. **Be open to how your messages come, where they come from, and who or what is delivering them**: The clues sometimes are within objects or in the environment around us. The messengers can be anyone: a clerk, cashier, delivery person, young child, an elder, or someone you're standing in line with. Stay on high alert, and those individuals will make themselves known.

5. **Give and be ready to receive**: Just as you are ready to get the information or guidance you are seeking, so are others. You never know when you will play an instrumental role in someone's life. Each of us has our own experiences and set of knowledge that others can learn from, and the more willing we are to share that, the more we attract others that are willing to do the same. The more you give, the more you will receive.

> "When you have wit of your own, it's a pleasure
> to credit other people for theirs."
> —Criss Jami, author of *Killosophy*

THE LETTER

Months later after leaving my desk job, I found my way to Parsons in New York City. I was finally at the point of the infamous interview that determines whether you get into the design department or not. As I sat anxiously in the waiting area outside of the conference room where the interviews took place, I scanned the room and saw black cases of all different sizes being guarded by each of their owners. I couldn't help but wonder, was mine big enough? Everyone else's seemed bigger or fancier than mine. As I impatiently waited, I was becoming more paranoid and started to doubt my decision of applying in the first place. I sat there nervously as the students before me were getting their portfolios scrutinized and ripped apart, one after the other. The conference room door was wide open so all those waiting for their names to be called could hear everything. It was finally my turn. I walked into the room with a confident stride, although my heart was racing out of control. I wasn't used to an admission decision being based on someone's personal opinion of my art skills and imagination. My grades and prior education allowed me to get to this step as I was already academically admitted. However, the acceptance into the design department was based solely on my artwork and sense of creativity.

The representative for the school sped through the first few pages without taking notice. I didn't take that as a good sign, and my heart started to sink. Then suddenly, she paused on one page. It was a self-portrait sketched with charcoal. The assignment was to draw yourself while staring into a mirror. For the first time, she looked up at me and smiled. She then began to ask me questions. In that moment, I thought to myself, I may actually have a chance. She then looked down and took her time to leaf through the remaining pages. When she was done, she said she was going to recommend me to the admissions committee for the design department. I was thrilled and sincerely thanked her before saying my goodbyes. As I exited the room and walked past the remaining candidates in the waiting area, I could not believe that I, Nova, with no prior art or design background, just passed the in-person interview at Parsons.

I had also applied to several other top design schools. It was early February, and a letter came in the mail. The envelope was from the Fashion Institute of Technology, the birthplace of so many great design talents such as Calvin Klein and Norma Kamali. It was arguably the number one school in the world for fashion training. The envelope was thin, so I was hesitant to open it. Curiosity was killing me, so I gently tore away at the flap. I pulled out the neatly folded letter and began to read it. Seconds later, the paper dropped to the floor as if in slow motion. It fell and bounced before settling into the carpet. My jaw was still open as I was trying to process their decision. The letter began with, "Congratulations, you have been accepted to the accelerated Fashion Design program at the Fashion Institute of Technology." That was as far as I got . . .

A week later I received my second letter. This one was from Parsons. I was again an ecstatic recipient of another unbelievable acceptance. The exhilaration I felt was as if someone told me I just won a multimillion-dollar jackpot. I couldn't have been happier to be accepted into the top two schools of my choice. Following those letters came other acceptances, as well as scholarship offers from other schools including Drexel University and Moore School of Art. Now, the decision of where to go came down between my number one and number two, FIT and Parsons. I decided to give it time as I had at least a month or two to get back to them.

I was still floating on cloud nine when leafing through the mail a couple of weeks later when I stopped to take note of a large blue and white package with five letters staring back at me . . . UCONN. My heart started racing. I was quickly reminded of my decision to apply to the University of Connecticut's PhD program in clinical psychology. I opened the package and began to read one of the documents inside. I should have been celebrating after what I read. I had just been granted a spot into the doctoral program coupled with a job offer and a full scholarship to one of the most competitive clinical programs in the country. That year, eight out of the thousands of applicants were offered a spot in the freshman class. This was nothing to take lightly. Instead, I suddenly felt very uneasy.

Yikes! I definitely wasn't prepared for this. I was overjoyed and confused at the same time. I was extremely grateful and in disbelief while saying to myself, *Now what*? How could I give up a lifetime opportunity like this, the chance to get my doctorate for free? I deeply loved the field of psychology and had always wanted to help people. On the other hand, I had just discovered my passion for design. This was arguably one of the toughest decisions I had to make.

SEVEN QUESTIONS TO SUPERNOVA CLARITY

Although I was just in my early twenties, I felt like I had lived a lifetime. The year following college graduation was a whirlwind. The "real world" was a rude awakening and forced me to reexamine what I wanted to do with the rest of my life. It was also a test of my will, determination, and self-confidence. Along the way, I asked myself six important questions to further justify the life-changing decision I made. The answers to these questions helped me find clarity and reaffirm that I was definitely on the right course, no matter how scary or uncertain it appeared to be. I share them with you below to further guide you through your own evolution and to help you more quickly find the answer to the big question: "What do you want to be when you grow up?"

1. **What's taking up your time?** I found myself spending 90 percent of my free time eating, sleeping, and breathing fashion. Even the psychology research I was doing revolved around human behavior as it related to communicating

through clothing and other visual cues. One of the major secrets to finding where your inner strength lies is to take note of what you love spending your time doing. No talent is bad. It only requires more grooming, skills, and practice to make it a creative entrepreneurship venture.

2. **What do you do regularly?** Since middle school, I found myself waking up every day with an excitement to wow my classmates with the newest outfit I put together. I recognized early on the power of style and creativity. The more creative I was, the more I made people smile and the more self-confident I became. My fashion sense helped me through those awkward teenage years. Being the new kid in school and one of the only girls with brown skin in each of my classes, fashion became one of my superpowers. Consistency is another key to unleash your talents and abilities. What you do often, whether consciously or not, comes from your inner supernova and those around you can feel it too. Therein lies your strength. Creative entrepreneurs look for ways to monetize the consistency of their talents and abilities. Starting now, list out things you do regularly or consistently without being cajoled into doing them. There is always a business side to it.

3. **What are you known for?** For as long as I can remember, I was known for the use of color and accessories in my outfits as well as dressing in unique designs. I always liked to keep people guessing with what I would wear. My friends came to me for fashion advice and those closest to me always looked forward to what I would wear at any major event. What your name represents to others is your cue to who they think you are. For example, Jake the photographer, Sheila the baker, Tom the artist, Luke the violinist. We might call that talented

friend by their given name officially but, subconsciously, we make reference to their creative abilities. What talents do you think you are known for? This is the beginning of your brand image. Just like any successful company, in time your brand builds loyalty and popularity and even monetary compensation for what it's best known for.

4. **What do you enjoy researching?** I have always been a researcher. Curiosity and a love for learning are both in my blood. However, some research is more exciting than others. I didn't have to wait for an assignment to begin researching the history of fashion, industry news, trendsetting designers, or the science behind the psychology of fashion. It was an activity that became a healthy obsession led simply by my personal interests. Research in terms of wanting to know more about a particular skill, idea, or hobby could be another key to self-discovery. Is there a particular area of interest you tend to read more about during your leisure time?

5. **What is your vision?** The day I made up my mind to pivot from my doctoral program to fashion design I had a clear vision to change the history of fashion and impact haute couture. This vision created the necessary steps to execute that dream. Design school gave me the skills and knowledge needed to launch my own fashion company and soon after be awarded Haute Couture Designer of the Year. The human mind is designed to have a mental picture of probable events that can happen in the future. The journey to self-actualization must come with a mental picture of what is attainable. Visualizing your goals gives you a clear direction of the best possible ways to achieve them. Without visualization, execution is slim. Most top achievers in the

world today started out as dreamers with an aim to become the top 1 percent in their field. Their visualization was so strong that it propelled them to execute every idea into reality.

6. **Is it the right time?** I used to feel that my deeply rooted academic life was a disadvantage to me at design school, but as I moved through the program, I noticed how it worked to my advantage in understanding sales, customer acquisitions, analytics, and much more. Therefore, I am grateful for my studies in clinical psychology and not having a traditional artistic path. I feel that my distinctive background and experience gave me the understanding and self-assurance I needed to become a successful creative entrepreneur. Timing is everything, but the key is to stay flexible and open to what appeals to you, and to realize that your goals might change. If they do, that's okay. If today you want to be an engineer and tomorrow you want to be a teacher, don't sweat it. Assess your needs in your current time and space and see which of those desires appeal to you most. To help in this process, make a list of what fulfills your needs and responsibilities most right now, then create a plan to weave in your other passion along the way.

7. **Are you being honest with yourself?** When I decided to take a sharp turn and not finish out my PhD, I knew there were people in my life that would be affected by my new career choice. It was important to me to communicate with them and have those difficult conversations in order to come to a resolution that I was happy with. Since most of us want to feel loved and accepted by those we admire most, it's important to allow ourselves the ability to be wholly committed to the choices we make. Some of us have to deal with the expectations of our

parents, our spouses, siblings, in-laws, or others. Do not hold back on your dreams even if you feel you're not living up to the expectations of those you love and are closest to.

W.O.W

Allow yourself to welcome the evolution.

CHAPTER FOUR

Sometimes, an unexpected turn of events leads you
to an unhappy place
and becomes the trigger for internal reflection.
In time, tears transform to joy
and suddenly you find your inner star.

~

IGNITING YOUR SUPERNOVA

Growing up with four brothers definitely had its advantages. Comics and superheroes were an everyday part of life. Although my brothers didn't have any Wonder Woman comic books around, I was lucky enough to watch her on TV and would find myself constantly thinking and pretending that I was just as strong as her and that my invisible jet could protect me from anything in the sky. Touching on the word sky, it seemed that I was always fascinated with it, making the name Nova very fitting for me. I grew up experiencing almost everyone who heard my name for the first time being intrigued by its uniqueness and galactic reference. Many then would follow with the question,

"Do you know what your name means?" Or, "Did you say Nova, as in supernova?"

A supernova is the explosion of a star in which the star may reach a maximum intrinsic luminosity one billion times that of the sun. It's incredible to know that something could become a billion times brighter than one of the most powerful things in nature. I thought to myself, *what if we equated that to ourselves*? Could this mean that tapping into my inner brilliance, known as my creative force, was the key to becoming the greatest version of myself? It would be decades before I could put all the pieces together and articulate what I was intuitively beginning to discover early on in my life's journey.

Now that I had discovered this inner force, I ignited it by first recognizing that I was a creative being and that my creativity was the seed to my dreams. I had to harness, protect, and then grow my creativity to its maximum potential. When choosing to become an entrepreneur, I was doing the same thing for my business. The struggle was always balancing the juggling act of staying inspired while scaling my ideas. The solution was never instant. It was a challenging yet fulfilling process.

> "The inner fire is the most important thing mankind possesses."
> —Edith Södergran

SIX WAYS TO IGNITE YOUR SUPERNOVA

1. **Own Your Talent:** It took years, but I finally became comfortable enough to admit that I was creative, good at designing, and very fashion savvy. Just the thought of telling stories through fabric, colors, and silhouettes really excited me. I

ignored these talents for a long time because I let my lack of experience and exposure to art and the fashion industry limit my personal validation of my gifts. Do you have a wonderful voice, know how to play a musical instrument, design intricate patterns, or build simple solutions to complex problems? There are many gifts that we are born with which we take for granted. Focus in on the one that brings a smile to your face, then think of a problem you have experienced and see if your gift can be a part of the answer. Zero in on this and don't ever feel embarrassed or apologetic about it.

2. **Keep Track of Your Ideas:** A teacher once told me to keep a notebook by my bed at night because the most creative ideas will come to me in my dreams. Nowadays my ideas are split between my notebooks and my phone's notepad. One dream became the beginning of a TV series and another became a screenplay, which I am now turning into a musical production for theater. No dream is too big to pursue. Anytime you conceive an idea, write it down. You never know which idea is the golden ticket to achieving your entrepreneurial dreams. Additionally, no idea is too small to be ignored. An open mind is the perfect receiver of great ideas, so avoid clouding your judgment with thoughts of impossibilities, fear, doubt, and impatience.

3. **Don't Be Reality's Fool:** I decided to be bold enough to apply to the world's best fashion design schools. This wouldn't have been a laughable notion if I had graduated from a top art school, but I was purely immersed in the sciences throughout my college years. If I allowed my current circumstances at the time to dictate my decision to move forward with my goals, I wouldn't have been brave enough to go after them. What we have or don't have in a present moment can deceive

us. It can paralyze us from believing that an idea is achievable. The step from conceiving that idea to making it into an achievable goal is an inner force known as our supernova. Dare to bring that idea into reality. Nothing is so unreal that it can't be manifested. Look within to see the possibilities and be determined to work hard on your ideas. Break them into action plans or milestones that can guide you on your journey to success. Ideas often come easy, it's the execution that stops most of us.

4. **Acknowledge Your Brilliance:** When I received acceptance letters from all of the schools that I applied to that year, both for design and for psychology, I could no longer ignore my brilliance. It wasn't something that I bragged or talked about. It was a feeling I internalized that drove me to work hard with confidence, one step at a time. It was the very thing that kept leading me through the most uncertain of opportunities. You are bright and super talented. Never let anyone tell you otherwise. Look deep within and identify that exceptionally good skill that is inside you. The more you execute that skill, the more knowledge and mastery you gain. Your brilliance is like a perfect work of art that can never be hidden, no matter how long it takes to develop it. Only those who believe in their abilities can truly be outstanding.

5. **Admit That You Are a Creative:** The closest I came to doing anything artistic while in undergraduate school was studying a different language in a foreign country and performing as part of a professional dance company. I didn't consciously connect either of these experiences to my sense of creativity. It wasn't until I decided to sit down and start sketching my designing ideas that I finally accepted my creative side. Creative persons are those who are highly imaginative and

invent original ideas to bring something incredibly amazing to the world. Human creativity is highlighted in many areas such as design, architecture, fashion, performing arts, advertising, communication, film, video, music, literature, and technology, to name just a few. Think of what you love to do. Maybe it's time for you to accept the truth of your own creative sensibility.

6. **Understand Creative Entrepreneurship:** In my twenties, I began to connect the dots and combine my love for helping people with my love for creativity. I made the decision to study entrepreneurship to develop the business skills needed to turn my passion into profit. Creative entrepreneurship is the process of setting up a business venture around your creative skills or abilities by taking risks and discovering opportunities within your niche. Creative entrepreneurs always seek ways to sell, invest in, and promote their talent because they have an overwhelming desire to bring value to their communities.

W.O.W

Don't deny what you know is your truth.

CHAPTER FIVE

Although the force of the wind was behind it,
the kite could not fly more than a few feet high.
That's because it never realized it was a kite.
It only saw itself as a patterned paper to decorate the sky.

WHAT DO YOU WANT TO BE?

At the age of thirteen, I started asking myself the age-old question, "What do you want to be when you grow up?" As a new teen, I loved doing hair. I was obsessed with learning about different hair products and flipping through new hair magazines for inspiration on the latest styles. At the time, I knew for sure that I wanted to become a hairdresser. Once I figured out the answer to this so important question, I went into the kitchen and shared the great news with my mom.

"Mommy?"

"Yes?" She responded.

"I know what I want to be when I grow up!" I could barely hold back my excitement. She smiled, and her eyes widened in anticipation with my answer. I then blurted out, "I want to be a hairdresser." Only silence followed. My mom had bigger career plans for me: doctor, lawyer, or nurse, perhaps. I could imagine these career options running through her mind. All were clearly in contrast to what I just stated.

Let me put this moment into perspective. My mom and dad emigrated from Jamaica to this country when they were in their early twenties. They brought four very young children with them, and I was the youngest. I didn't remain the youngest for too long as my younger brother and sister eventually followed. The whole reason they left their birthplace and family and friends behind was to make a better life for their family. Coming from a traditional Jamaican family, most career plans were pretty straightforward. They mainly consisted of the options above with the addition of engineer and teacher. Creative pursuits were seen as hobbies, not careers.

Instantly, I could see the worried look on my mom's face as she likely thought, *Oh no, does that mean she will not go to college? Will she make enough money to support herself or to help support her family*? However, she never voiced any of these opinions. After a few moments of silence, she answered with a half-smile and a soft voice, "That's nice." That very moment was the end of my desire to become a hairdresser.

FINDING THE ANSWER

In hindsight, I'm actually glad my mother gave me the response she did. Although I loved playing with hair, I learned later that this was more of a hobby rather than a purpose. What makes us happy as a teenager could be very different from what gives us joy in our forties. Our wants and desires change as we do.

Some of us may carry childhood ideals or pursuits that never go away, but even then, those wishes tend to evolve as we grow, and that's okay. I have come to realize that four major components drive us to answer the all-important question we started off with. Understanding the key elements behind our decisions will bring us closer to where we are supposed to be.

1. **Change**: The first step in discovering what you want to be when you grow up is to accept that what you want is going to be directly related to what makes you happy. If what makes you happy changes as the years pass, commit now to being okay with these changes. Each year that passes, we carry a new set of experiences with us. We meet several new people and encounter many more firsts that offer opportunities for growth and evolution. We learn more about ourselves and what we like versus what we love. These realizations and discoveries are essential to pinpointing the right doors for each step in life. Embracing the personal expansion that comes with change is a major leap forward in the right direction.

2. **Belief Systems**: Recognize that a lot of stress or anxiety comes from our belief systems. We don't want to disappoint those that are closest to us, especially if they sacrificed a lot of their time or resources for us. Another possible belief is that we don't want to seem like a flake or a failure. Being indecisive is not always looked upon very favorably by our peers. Therefore, we stick with one answer just because that was the answer we came up with some years ago and are too afraid to admit that we changed our mind.

3. **Happiness**: If you don't have a definitive answer to what you want to be, you may feel alone, inadequate, and possibly afraid. In those moments, what do we do? We have to always

stay true to who we are. This is something that shouldn't waver. If we focus on what makes us happy in the present moment, it will guide us to the next step.

4. **Honesty**: Start having open discussions with those you care about and be honest about what is important to you. Find a middle ground at whatever stage you are in. All experiences are valuable experiences.

Deciding what you want to become in the future is one of the most important questions you could ever ask yourself. This question can take you on a journey of self-realization that can help you discover your purpose in life. What do you see yourself doing in a short bit of time, medium amount of time, or a long duration of time? This will give you a mental picture of your most desired activities for the coming weeks, months, and years.

> "Our job in this life is not to shape ourselves into some ideal we imagine we ought to be, but to find out who we already are and become it."
> —Steven Pressfield, *The War of Art*

LEAVING CERTAINTY FOR THE UNKNOWN

Having just received an incredible offer letter from the University of Connecticut, I was really torn with the decision to pursue my PhD in clinical psychology or a fashion degree from one of the top design schools in the world. I needed time to think. This new change of events was a blessing, but also a sudden burden. Should I continue the path that I had been on for years, a sure route to helping people, financial security, and societal acceptance? Or should I take a leap of faith into a field I knew nothing about, powered only by pure intuition and desire, while risking ridicule and rejection?

I took a couple of weeks to weigh the pros and cons. At the end of the second week, I made up my mind. I convinced myself that continuing the path I was on was the best choice for me. After all, how else could I better help people than through academic research and one-on-one counseling? I could use the data and clinical experience, coupled with my diverse background, to really add a unique perspective to the field and make a considerable impact. I told myself that this fashion thing could wait. I always wanted to be a doctor and here was my chance. I could always do fashion when I retire.

Just like that, I was back on track to becoming a doctor. I signed my UCONN offer letter and put it in the mail. I should have felt elated. Truthfully, part of me was, but the other part felt some heavy rocks in the bottom of my stomach. It took a few more days to respond back to all of the other programs. I was perhaps thinking I could somehow do both. I knew this was just comedic thinking, but it helped me numb myself to the difficult decision I just made. Before I sent off my responses to the design programs, a thought came to me. This definitely was divinely sent. Something I grew to learn happens quite often to me. *Why not defer your acceptance at your top choice*? I asked myself. Both FIT and Parsons offered the option of delaying your enrollment for a year. It was a silly notion because I just committed to a four-year doctoral program. *It doesn't matter, I have nothing to lose and at least I won't immediately burn any bridges,* I thought to myself.

Well, that decided it. I was on my way to graduate school. As the concept sunk in, I started to get more and more excited as the first day of school drew closer and closer. I was always fascinated by human behavior and the mind. I started to see that I had more and more things to get excited about and my urgent need to pursue fashion design started to fade.

~

The school year was finally here. I was one of eight in my freshman class. It was a completely different experience from undergrad with the smallest class size being twenty-five to thirty students. The classes were all very interesting and the workload was considerable. I was content, and I saw this new phase in my life as a huge milestone for my family and me.

It only took me about a month or two to settle into my new routine before I started drifting back to the possibility of becoming a fashion designer. For weeks, I couldn't shake the following thoughts from my head: *You have to go to New York. You have to study fashion.* I started to experience shortness of breath and rapid heart palpitations with no warning. After a quick checkup, I was told that I needed to examine anything weighing heavily on my mind that could express itself physically like this. Of course, I instantly knew what it was. I knew it was time to acknowledge the fact that this was a very real desire that I could no longer neglect.

After that day, I had an epiphany about my future. As I stood outside the main campus building, a vision came to me and stopped me right in my tracks. I will explain it the best way I can because even when I think about it now it still seems so supernatural.

It was early fall in Connecticut. The copper, crimson, and mustard color leaves were in full bloom on the trees. I took the usual path from my car to the three-story brick building that my morning class was held in. The walk is usually no more than about five to ten minutes, just long enough to get a taste of the crisp air and smell of the fallen leaves. Something was different this morning. I walked a little slower than usual. Those that know me are not surprised by the brisk pace I have when walking, probably a lingering after-effect of cross-country running for so many years. I think it's also directly related to the cold seasons, for, as a native Jamaican, my body never quite adjusted to temperatures below 60 degrees. Looking back, my slower than usual pace was definitely a foreshadowing of the event that was about to change everything.

I finally arrived in front of my class building. However, I didn't quickly enter to get out of the cold. Instead, I paused about thirty feet in front of the wide metal door. I felt as if I couldn't move, as if something was forcing me to stand still in that place. Then, out of nowhere, an image of the hallways and classrooms with my classmates standing in them appeared to me. It was as if I was right there observing them and their conversations and even their future conversations. I saw what life would be like if I stayed or if I left. I felt that this was not the path for me. I was then taken to another vision. Imagine standing stage left and looking at yourself talking or interviewing someone on stage with an audience in front of you. This was the scene I saw. At that moment, I knew that somehow that second vision was how I was going to help people, a lot of people. However, that is all I knew. I had no idea what it had to do with psychology or even fashion. What I took away from it was a very strong desire to end my psychology studies early and make what some people would call a crazy decision: leave the dream of becoming a doctor for a new dream of becoming a designer.

After that profoundly unusual experience, I knew what I needed to do. I went home that day with a plan. I would complete my masters in clinical psychology in one year and then transition to the Fashion Institute of Technology. Once settling on this new strategy, I was finally at peace. In the days and weeks and months following, all of my free time was spent in the bookstore and library studying as much as I could about past designers and their techniques. New York couldn't come soon enough, and my family was equally excited for my new adventure.

W.O.W

Once we stop trying to lock ourselves into just one interest, the magic begins.

CHAPTER SIX

I do it because I love it.

~

NOT YOUR AVERAGE LOVE AFFAIR

Now that you have all the answers to your why and what you want to do, creating a new business, product, or service is the logical next step. In other words, entrepreneurship. Getting to know the reality of this path as soon as possible is a necessity in enduring the marathon.

FIVE LESSONS A PAPER ROUTE CAN TEACH YOU

My first taste of the entrepreneurial life was an apprenticeship as an assistant paper girl. My trial run with delivering papers began while apprenticing under my older brothers, who graciously paid me one dollar per week for my services (which was 20 percent of their weekly earnings, believe it or not)! Getting up at the crack of dawn while still having to catch my 7:00 a.m. school bus, even in the dead of winter, didn't deter me, even though I was barely nine years old when I started my paper route stewardship. What got me out of bed in the pitch-dark cold mornings was the fact that I loved the idea of working alongside my older brothers. It felt great to be trusted with such an important task at a young age.

When I was old enough, I chose to get my own paper route. This meant that I was committed to my daily responsibilities, no matter the weather, 365 days a year. Although the pay was meager starting out, it directly increased due to my efforts of consistency, friendliness, and timeliness. That is what entrepreneurship is all about. Here are the five things I learned from my paper route that still ring true for me today:

1. I may strongly dislike some of the tasks that come with the job.
2. I may be alone sometimes and have to carry a heavy burden.
3. I may not make as much money as I want at first, but if I stick to it, I eventually will.
4. I have to get a product delivered to my customers on time and in good quality.
5. I have to learn to both understand and love the process to succeed.

My paper route was a brief introduction to learning to love the good, bad, and ugly of what it means to be an entrepreneur. Apprenticeships like this allow kids and teens to develop the hands-on skills needed for entrepreneurship in real time and expose more people to the possibility of becoming an entrepreneur early on.

> "A rock pile ceases to be a rock pile the moment a single man contemplates it, bearing within him the image of a cathedral."
> —Antoine de Saint-Exupery, author of *The Little Prince*

~

I was off to the races and successfully raised enough money from family and friends to create my very first fashion line. It's funny when I think about it now because during that time in my life I thought I knew everything there was to know about starting a fashion business. My preparation included fashion school and working in a few industry jobs to get a sense of the dos and don'ts of a successful business. I even took courses in marketing and got certified in entrepreneurship. What else was there to know? A whole lot!

The first public look at my creations was alongside the Hudson River in Westchester, New York. Going back to that beautiful sunny day in September, it couldn't have been a more perfect setting. I had family and friends fly in from all over for my debut fashion show. It would be one of many shows that I would go on to produce, and it was a huge success! The proof of concept worked, and my designs were loved by all, but what I quickly learned in that first year of business is that it takes more than a well-liked product to create and grow a profitable venture. The product is just the beginning.

What I didn't have prepared was a solid sales plan or a team of experienced salespeople. I also didn't account for the many all-nighters I would have to pull to juggle both motherhood and entrepreneurship. I had two babies when I launched my fashion company and was still nursing my youngest. Thank goodness for moms and dads as both of mine were integral in me sustaining my wits that first year in business. They would drive an hour and half every Sunday to help with the kids and cook a big meal for our family of four. My mom would stay for the week and my dad would drive back home that Sunday evening to ready for work the next day. My mom being there during the week helped me attend meetings and events in New

York city that would come up sporadically, often with a day's notice or less.

Although I had the support of my parents as it related to helping me care for our two little ones, I still needed to raise over two million dollars to launch my company, so I set off to find my angel investor. Remembering the advice I received years prior, I shared my plans with every stranger I met who cared to listen. When you are passionate about something to the point that it radiates out of you every time you talk about it, people will feel that energy and share that same excitement back in their interest to truly help or support you. I am so very grateful for everyone who took a chance on me that year. Those conversations led to penthouse parties in Manhattan, my first client sale, invitations to exclusive resorts to sell my clothing, meeting celebrities such as Johnny Cochran, selling his wife one of my designs, and getting a request from him to see my business plan. That first year was a whirlwind which included some big disappointments as well.

One included an angel investor that promised a store on Madison Avenue for me and four other hand-picked rising designers with money for our production, sales, and promotion. After months of meetings and negotiations, conversations dried up as well as the opportunity, as this person proved to be a very passionate fake. Another introduction led me to a very savvy business owner who presented himself as a caring mentor and offered some great advice, but I followed my gut and did nothing with the information shared. I was contacted by the FBI years later when they found a file with my name on it in his office while raiding his office for fraud. They contacted me to make sure I wasn't one of his victims and went on their merry way. This is something that school does not teach you. When networking, it is extremely important to surround yourself with people who have your best interests at heart that you can discuss offers, contracts, or any other guidance that strangers provide you with.

Another lesson I learned in my first year of business is that choosing the right team members is critical to the success of whatever you do. This is most obvious in sports. For example, the right point guard, center, or shooting guard can make a good basketball team exceptional. Being a part of UCONN's cheer squad during the meteoric rise of their men's and women's basketball teams was a one-of-a-kind adventure and an amazing opportunity for me to learn this lesson firsthand. Unfortunately, while cheering I was paying more attention to the wins than on the strategy. It took years to incorporate this lesson into my own business, and I paid the price by hiring for the wrong staffing roles, which cost me over one-hundred thousand dollars in losses.

My first year in business continued to come with rejection after rejection from venture capitalists (VCs) and angel investors, even with the perfect business plan. The nos helped me realize a few things:

- The perfect business plan doesn't always attract the money you need.
- Never wait on anyone to give you permission to proceed.
- Money isn't everything—intention and patience are.

Try to view entrepreneurship as a game and know that the unpredictability of how things play out is part of the fun and excitement. If you try not to take the ups and downs so seriously, you can more easily sustain the bumps along the way. Allow the belief in your idea to guide you and be open to how it can come to life. Where I started and what I thought I wanted are very different from where I am now, but I am very happy with how things have unfolded. I have grown along the way and found ways to share my love for helping others while exploring news areas of my creativity outside of fashion.

FIVE MYTH-BUSTERS OF ENTREPRENEURSHIP

1. **You don't make your own hours**: Depending on your industry, monetary goals, or product, you work as long as it takes to get the job done. If it takes six months to develop a prototype, then that is what it will take for a time commitment, especially in the beginning stages. Entrepreneur, author, speaker, and Internet personality Gary Vaynerchuk recommends that new entrepreneurs work eighteen hours a day in their first year. Some work sixty hours a week on a regular basis. Your business niche as well as your personal circumstances will further define when and how much you work.

2. **It's not all roses and rainbows**: When I had my paper route, I had to deal with inclement weather, dark and cold mornings, and heavy bags that had to be delivered by foot for miles. It wasn't fun most of the time, but the joy of helping and being with my brothers while earning my own cash along the way was worth it.

3. **It's a marathon, not a sprint**: You need resolve and perseverance. There is sweat and grunt work involved, menial tasks, and long days. It often takes more than four or five years, not weeks or months, before achieving success. Also, when creating something new and different, not everyone will instantly support or hire you. Rejection seems to be more common than not. Days, weeks, and months of juggling multiple responsibilities can also wear you out. Mentally and physically preparing yourself for a journey and not a quick sprint will greatly help.

4. **The VC route is not for most**: According to Fundable.com, only .05 percent of startups get venture capital funds, which

means that 99.95 percent have to find the stick-to-itiveness to get through the days of little to no cash flow. Thankfully, there are other ways to build a business without a VC. Focus your attention on developing a sound business model from the ground up. If you want a billion-dollar business, develop a plan for one and spend a lot of time discovering a variety of means to financially support and grow your business in its early stages.

5. **It takes more than an idea**: An instructor once asked our entrepreneurship class the first question you should ask yourself before writing your business plan. Most of our class responded but no one had the answer she was looking for. Her reply to us was, "Decide how much you need or want to make, and build a solid business model around that." She further stated that if you are not happy with how much you are making, no idea alone can sustain you in the long run. Launching a visionary idea in order to make an impact on those around you and taking it through to execution requires a variety of skills and knowledge—all of which may not be apparent to the majority of people in the early stages of their endeavor. Most idealists look to other successful entrepreneurs that have come before them, but they usually don't hear about the not-so-sexy stages that got their favorite business personality from the starting point to the finish line. This further motivated me to put my experiences and knowledge to paper, to serve as a go-to guide for those that get stuck or need an extra push along the way. Still trying to decide if you should take a shot at entrepreneurship?

~

Entrepreneurship isn't for everybody, though if you carry the desire for more freedom and creating income for yourself, it can lead you to living the life of your dreams. Entrepreneurship can afford you the ability to create the lifestyle you want, helping you follow your passion, while allowing you to work for yourself. A dream can become a reality due to the efforts made to transform an idea into a workable plan.

Entrepreneurship shouldn't be taken lightly. It entails a lot of sacrifice, commitment, and time. It's also important to mention that entrepreneurship is not the promise of unlimited cash. In addition to acquiring the needed funding to kick-start their business, entrepreneurs cannot rely solely on a check that will pay the bills. To survive entrepreneurship, you need to maintain enthusiasm, duty, satisfaction, and development.

However, for those that love the process of using their gifts to impact those around them, the rewards far outweigh the challenges. Entrepreneurs can make what they need become achievable and bring to life the vision of accomplishing something one of a kind. On this journey, they can surround themselves with like-minded people and create a motivated team all while finding happiness in doing the things that they love. Sometimes we hear successful entrepreneurs say, "Every day is a holiday when you are doing what you love." They are highly innovative, dedicated, and often do extraordinary things which set them apart from the crowd.

W.O.W

If you can do the grunt work, you're halfway there.

CHAPTER SEVEN

It's important to pack the right gear to successfully reach the top of the mountain.

~

THE CLIMB UP MOUNT ENTREPRENEURSHIP

The paper route was just a brief taste of the world I soon found myself in as a young adult. Although extremely helpful, it did not prepare me for the meat and potatoes of running a business. I was unaware of the issues that came with being young, having no track record, no team, and dealing with naysayers, loneliness, stereotypes, and stress. These are topics that I wish I learned prior to starting my first company.

I was in my twenties, full of ambition, drive, and energy . . . or at least I thought. I honestly believe that being in a boxing ring and choosing to get back up after each major blow is a good description of what this roller-coaster ride felt like at times. I was a new mom with another on the way, working a full-time job, and trying to get my first business loan of five hundred dollars. It might as well have been five thousand. For any entrepreneur, getting anyone, let alone a lending institution, to believe in you enough to invest any amount of money is one of the most wonderful senses of accomplishments.

After the completion of my entrepreneurship certification course and submission of my business plan, my loan was awarded by Fighting Poverty with Microfinance and Social Enterprise (FINCA), an organization that focuses on micro-loans for women-owned businesses. If I successfully paid off the loan, I would be granted double the amount the next round with a positive reporting to my credit. There were three rounds in total. It was my first step of many on the climb up Mount Entrepreneurship. It helped me overcome one of the biggest challenges, building a financial track worth and credit history to open doors for more capital when I needed to grow. However, many more obstacles lay before me. Let's delve a little deeper into the most common obstacles that hold entrepreneurs back.

SEVEN OBSTACLES TO ENTREPRENEURSHIP

1. No Financial Track Record

One of the most common challenges experienced by any entrepreneur is the issue of finances. More seasoned and older entrepreneurs have the benefit of building an impressive credit history which makes it easier for them to get loans and investors. A newbie or younger entrepreneur cannot brag about having all of these resources because it takes time to build them. Because of your limited access to financial capital, you have fewer chances for mistakes to happen. Ensure that you have enough money set aside to help you through the tough times. Furthermore, don't expect to profit from your business immediately. It can take a minimum of two years before your business is profitable. Growing a business as a young entrepreneur is totally possible, yet having an organized and tested strategy is very important in order to kick off on a positive note.

2. Stereotypes

Unfortunately, people may judge you based on their own preconceived business notions. As it relates to being of a younger age when starting a business, for example, you might be regarded as naive or inexperienced and not be taken as seriously as somebody who is more established. Try not to give ageism or any other stereotype a chance to get to you. Focus instead on moving forward with your dreams and continue to always put positivity first. Most importantly, trust in your very own abilities to build the business of your dreams.

3. Loneliness

In the process of building your business, it can be difficult to keep up with social events and opportunities. As a new entrepreneur, you may not have colleagues to visit with, and your loved ones may not really understand the entrepreneurial route you have taken. With the demands of your schedule, it can also be difficult to get out and meet new individuals or keep up with your current relationships. Fortunately, there are other young business visionaries out there who are in a similar situation. In the end, there is a powerful effect of being surrounded by people who will constantly encourage you rather than tear you down. Putting your energy on the positive people in your life makes it a lot simpler to develop the business of your dreams.

4. Criticism

People don't always have faith in anyone that wants to start their own business until they are successful. Sometimes it's hard not to take the negative feedback personally, but always take time to separate good criticism from the bad. Don't squander your time focusing on the negative comments.

5. Stress

Building your own business can be very stressful. In contrast to working for an employer, there's no manager to report to when things turn sour. Normal exercise and meditation can help relax you and calm your brain. Furthermore, as your own boss, you are allowed to take a quick break at whatever point you like and change your work setting to help you relax. If the stress is getting to you and you feel like giving up, look at how far you have come and what the future holds.

6. Finding the Right Team

Finding or hiring employees can be a daunting assignment for a young businessperson. You're searching for someone with not only the talent to do the job but also the trustworthiness and shared passion for the cause. Let's not forget that you need all of this within a budget you can afford. To minimize risk, start with freelancers or consultants. These individuals can turn into the best team member down the line. Another solution is to work with an employment agency that can help you filter and manage your new hire. As you grow your business, work hard at creating a culture that people would want to brag about to their friends and family. It should be an environment that embodies the very qualities that attracted you to entrepreneurship in the first place. Soon, people will be finding and asking you for employment opportunities.

7. Getting Customers

When acquiring new customers, home in on the demographic, geographic, and psychographic profile of your ideal consumer. Then, figure out how to find the consumer and how your offering best fits their life. This will also allow you to better analyze if you are truly providing value. A marketing budget is usually an afterthought for most entrepreneurs but should really be top priority. It can be the cost of getting you to and from networking events, digital ad campaigns, and developing a strong social presence or captivating website. If you have the mindset of giving before receiving, such as sending out freebies, limited time offers, and customized bundled packages, you will show your audience that your value far outweighs the price. Pay attention to your brand story and how it can impact your customer and motivate them to purchase something from you. This is just the start of your rewarding journey as an independent entrepreneur.

> "To live a creative life, we must lose our fear of being wrong."
> —Joseph Chilton Pearce

HOW TO UNLOCK YOUR CREATIVE ABILITIES

Discover: The key to creativity is the revelation point at which you become mindful of or unearth something that was not in existence before. Discovering your creative potential can help you link abstract concept into a possible reality. To discover your creative abilities, allow yourself time off from your typical everyday practice. Tune in to new music, attempt abnormal activities, visit a fascinating store, break out from the norm, and experience your reality in out-of-the-box ways. If you need to make music, listen to the groups you appreciate. If you need to paint, make an accumulation of the considerable number of specialists and works that overwhelm you. Motivation is one of the greatest helpers in masterful creativity.

Analyze: Creative abilities are strengthened through analysis. When I need to make financial decisions, I run analysis to help me discover how to spend less and earn more. As a creative entrepreneur, I analyze the best way to portray the talents and skills of others to motivate and inspire my audience.

Develop: As a creative entrepreneur, always remember that no idea is too vague to become a reality. Oftentimes we overlook certain ideas because we feel that they do not have that wow factor, but in reality, there is uniqueness in every idea—it may just require a little work to make it outstanding. For instance, famous inventor Levi Strauss developed blue jeans when his client requested some solid jeans that could withstand hard labor work without tearing or easily wear out. Today, everywhere you go you will find someone wearing a pair of jeans. Development of ideas is one of the best ways to unlock your creative abilities; it is an exercise of your mental capabilities.

Mimic: Taking a cue from others can be an awesome method to develop as an entrepreneur. For instance, Orville and Wilbur Wright invented the airplane by mimicking the features and characteristics of birds in the sky. The airplane has since turned into a military device, a method for business transportation, and more. Creativity can be unlocked simply by mimicking the things that interest us most.

W.O.W

Challenges are just bumps in the road as a reminder that the strongest car will always outlast the fastest one.

CHAPTER EIGHT

Just when you think you made up your mind,
the wind of change comes back again.

~

WHAT'S YOUR ARCHETYPE?

I was born to be a creative entrepreneur. Looking back, entrepreneurship had always run through my veins. Growing up, I watched my Jamaican parents each hold down full-time jobs while opening and managing a very elegant lounge called the Ritz Café. This is the place they could commune with like-minded individuals that also loved to get dressed up and hear the top reggae and R&B hits, all while carrying on with lively conversation.

The Ritz became my first adult run at launching an idea to execution. During the first year of pursuing my PhD, my parents approached my husband and I to partner with them to rebrand and relaunch the Ritz Café. They knew it had a lot more potential and wanted to inject some new life into the well-known local social lounge. I quickly accepted the challenge, considering the only other business I ran before that was my neighborhood paper route when I was in middle school, but this was quite different from a paper route, and right up my alley. I was put in charge of redesigning the interior, finding talent for the live shows, and marketing and promotion.

I loved every moment spent researching the inspiration and theme of the new Ritz. We went with an old glam feel with bold geometric shapes and rich maroons accented with black and white tiled floors. We painted the tin ceiling black and added wood trim and paint to all the walls. We then brought in chic and elegant tables that encouraged intimate conversation with good views of the dance floor, which doubled as a staging area for the shows. I really enjoyed coming up with the promotions, flyers, and radio ads, but searching for talent was the icing on the cake. I found designers from Boston along with poets from larger cities. The Ritz was transformed into a relaxed social environment for the twenty- to thirty-somethings who appreciated fashion, jazz, and the spoken word. It didn't take long before word of the grand reopening had spread and the lounge became packed night after night. It was exhilarating being a part of a team and working to bring a common vision to life.

What I didn't anticipate was how hard it would be to walk away when it came time to move to New York to start my fashion program at F.I.T. My parents were equally sad when moving day actually came. However, they were very appreciative of all the work that went into repositioning the Ritz Café for a fresh start. Within that year, my parents were able to successfully sell the lounge. What I learned from that brief period in my life is that creativity and entrepreneurship go hand and hand. To take just a thought and turn it into a physical thing, be it a product or service that benefits others, is a tremendous act of creation. It takes flexibility, faith, drive, determination, and a whole lot of fun to bring about the best version of that thought. This is what I experienced as a co-collaborator in the Ritz project.

I have seen this sentiment echoed in the many interviews I have conducted as editor in chief of *Raine Magazine.* When I asked fellow entrepreneur Keith Kirkland, co-founder of WearWorks, how he would describe a creative entrepreneur in his own words, he replied with this incredible insight:

> A creative entrepreneur looks toward other industries for inspiration. They are well versed in a multitude of fields and draw from parallels or components in other areas to solve the problems in their own area of interest. As all work is "creative" by nature, because it requires creating, I personally feel all entrepreneurs are creative. They build imaginary worlds that don't yet exist for people that may not be able to see that the new world is, hopefully, better than the current one. They are storytellers, technologists, artists, activists, and caretakers. And they have a deep-seated belief that the world they envision is a world worth betting their livelihoods, and sometimes their lives, to build. As an entrepreneur, their role is to find a need and then to both develop and promote solutions that satisfy that need for a particular group of people, i.e. a market. While trying to address that need, a creative entrepreneur runs into every conceivable problem imaginable. But in lieu of those problems, or perhaps because of them, they sharpen their wit and their will and draw on something deeper that magnifies the potential of their original solution by orders of magnitude. They don't just create products; they create support systems that once born allow their creative solutions to flourish.

Regardless of whether independently employed or working in a particular industry, creative entrepreneurs utilize both the left and right sides of their brain to generate income. They do not need to be specialists; they are pioneers that get thoughts going. Some creative entrepreneurs include the following professions: craftsman, photographer, jeweler, graphic artist, blogger, musician, interior designer, fashion designer, actor, hair stylist, cartoon artist, prop stylist, writer, makeup artist, web designer, event planner, baker, video producer, painter, card designer, carpenter, music teacher, voice artist, calligrapher, event host, model, basket maker, florist, and so many more. I have described the most common archetypes of creative entrepreneurs below. Do you relate to any of these archetypes?

- **The Creative Collective**: Creative prodigies are in and of the world, and they come together to form one, like Voltron, to become even more powerful in their ability to disrupt and innovate responsibly. They are self-selected. No one can appoint them; they can only be inspired to appoint themselves.
- **Artistic Mastermind**: These creatives transform their insight and abilities into an entrepreneurship venture that pays. The artistic mastermind has authority over work, enjoys flexibility, and can plan their profession in line with their creative objectives. They take advantage of their range of abilities to earn a living.
- **Inventor**: The world has benefited from the imaginations and inventions of creative entrepreneurs. A standout is inventor Thomas Edison, who developed the electric light. Today, there are a great many numbers of not-so-famous creative inventors.
- **Educator**: These idea leaders have gained a lot of knowledge and experience in a particular creative field. They

mentor up-and-coming creatives on how to be successful in a chosen field. Great educators always know how to engage their audience.

- **Freelancer:** These creative entrepreneurs use their skills to make a living based on hourly rates or one-time payments; they are specialists in their field. Freelancing incorporates an assortment of occupations like website development, copywriting, video production, photography, digital marketing, and more. Freelancers tend to love having control of their time and skills.
- **Artist**: These individuals identify with making workmanship, rehearsing human expressions, or exhibiting their talents and abilities such as drawing, painting, form, acting, composing, filmmaking, photography, and music. The way to their prosperity is through artistic expression.
- **Entertainer**: These creative entrepreneurs utilize an assortment of media like digital broadcasts, YouTube recordings, podcasts, websites, and music to keep their fans engaged and subscribing to their services. Their key to their prosperity is building an audience of genuine fans that can afford to pay any amount to keep up with them. These creative entrepreneurs are known to bring laughter and relaxation to their fans.

Not many people refer to themselves as a creative entrepreneur but instead identify with one of the archetypes above. Whether you're a writer, an inventor, or an entertainer, the challenges are similar, and the goal is the same: to create. Use these archetypes as a guide to help you find your creative community and sustain you along this journey.

> "Let your creative and imaginative mind run freely; it will take you places you never dreamed of and provide breakthroughs that others once thought were impossible."
> —Idowu Koyenikan, author of *Wealth for All*

A GREEN TEAM AND AN UNFINISHED DREAM

My large and close-knit family taught me the value of teamwork. My parents were in a new country, raising children in an educational system they were unfamiliar with, all while adapting to a new culture. Our nucleus totaled eight, so getting along with each other was a necessity, not a choice. Since there were four of us that were very close in age, we often paired up in teams of two when needed. This dynamic of working in teams deeply influenced how I interact in a collaborative setting today. Teams are an integral part of idea generation for entrepreneurs. Often the idea starts with one person, but it is the effort of multiple minds coming together that can make a mere idea into a genius invention, concept, or business.

From an entrepreneurial perspective, my team experience started in design school. There were five of us, a very eclectic group of young women who came together and brought our different talents and expertise to the table. We all took on different roles in the group: visionary, technical designer, stylist, marketer, and operations manager. The five of us filled a significant place within the company and respected each other for what we offered. This is a critical component of early success when launching an entrepreneurial venture. In addition to our skill sets, we all shared the same love of fashion with a desire to bring clothing with a purpose to the market. When collaborating with a team, it is important that all parties are working toward the same goal.

Months after conceptualizing our plan, I found out I was expecting my first child and decided to rejoin my husband who was completing his training in another state. At first, I wasn't worried that anything would change with the team when I moved, because we came so far in our planning and were very close to beginning the first run of clothing samples for our fashion line. However, to my surprise, it only took about four to six weeks after my departure to witness the unraveling of our once solid team. A big lesson learned, without all team members present in the early stages, a company cannot survive.

WHAT SHOULD YOU CONSIDER BEFORE JOINING A TEAM?

1. What of value are you bringing to the existing group?
2. Do your skills complement or duplicate those of anyone else on the team?
3. What do you love most about this team and is it enough to commit long-term?
4. Are you more productive in a setting of two or more or does this type of environment take away from your creativity?
5. If someone else is leading the team, do you respect them and their vision?
6. Do your goals align with the mission of the project?
7. Are you critical of others?
8. Do you have strong verbal and written communication skills or willing to develop them?
9. Do you have prior team experience?
10. Are you flexible with change and okay with not always getting your own way?

Teamwork can yield amazing results if team members have the right chemistry. However, working in a team is not for everyone.

Consider the points above when contemplating if this will be a part of your own entrepreneurial journey.

W.O.W

Surround yourself with team members that both respect each other and balance each other out.

CHAPTER NINE

Each of us are born with a candle
just waiting to be lit.

~

THE FIVE AHAS OF FINDING YOUR BRILLIANCE

What do you want to be when you grow up? This is one of life's biggest quandaries. Most of us have been asked this question at least once in childhood. If it wasn't by our parents, it was by an aunt, uncle, teacher, or friend. As children, we usually blurt out whatever answer comes to our young mind. Usually, it's something common such as a doctor or lawyer (or YouTuber) and that becomes our label for the rest of our childhood life. I think this question should continue to be asked throughout our adulthood because I believe many of us still haven't figured it out or are discovering that there are many things we want to be depending on when the question is asked. It's a question I enjoy asking when doing interviews for *Raine Magazine*.

When I asked Christina Chironna, co-founder and COO of FilmUp, she said, "When I grow up, no matter what I'm doing

I want to be a light for others. I want to be free to create art that touches the human spirit. I want to be constantly learning, evolving and inspiring through my work, whether that be a company, film, painting, speech and so on. People are my inspiration, and I hope to inspire them too."

What would your response be? In our youth, we reply with the pressure of meeting the expectations of the person asking the question. If it's our grandparent, perhaps it is a title of prestige. If it's our schoolmate, our response may be something that is considered cool in that moment. It's important to remember that by design we are not singular beings. We are all multifaceted individuals with a variety of interests, talents, and experiences. For example, when my youngest son was two years old, he expressed an interest in becoming a "cooker," or at least that's what he called it then. Now, at fourteen years old, he makes breads, sauces, and cakes all from scratch. He experiments with recipes from various cultures including Thai, Indian, Chinese, Mexican, and, of course, Jamaican. He's never strayed from his interest in cooking. He now says he wants to be a chef. He has learned that he also loves storytelling, inventing, and engineering (and just finished writing his first book)! Some of these interests could nicely fit together as a career and some not so much. Keeping this in mind, we've been careful not to box him into choosing just one aspiration, instead allowing him to see for himself which of those interests stay true and which ones come to pass. When we try to force ourselves to focus on only one aspect of who we are, we deny the many layers that define us and the uniqueness of our multidimensional selves.

For those of us who feel compelled to follow the path that our young selves committed to in childhood, we can end up in an endless loop in adulthood, seeking to find our authentic selves. How many of us have asked a parent, relative, or friend what they would choose to be or do in life if they could do it all over? Most would share that it would be a different path from what they took or are currently on, and the lucky ones will gleefully answer, "I wouldn't change a thing."

Who we are at five or ten or fifteen is very different from who we will be at twenty-five, thirty-five, or even fifty-five. Our adolescent needs are very different from our adult needs. What fulfills us at any age is unique to where we are in life. As we grow, we gain experiences, build relationships, and develop new skills and interests that can change throughout our lifetime.

~

UNLOCKING YOUR INNER BRILLIANCE

Unlocking your inner brilliance as a creative entrepreneur is using the act of imagination to develop a totally unique concept that would meet extraordinary demands and therefore gain high market acceptance. Unlocking your inner brilliance is only possible when you have mastery of your SWOT (**S**trengths, **W**eaknesses, **O**pportunities, **T**hreats) and make a conscious effort to put this knowledge into action. Here are five important practices to help unlock your inner brilliance:

Problem-Solving: The core of entrepreneurship is problem-solving. Most of the time we are tempted to walk away from our challenges rather than find solutions to them. History has shown that successful entrepreneurs have time and again learned to solve world problems and as a result are able to reap profitable rewards. Your brilliance can make a fortune if you choose to face difficult tasks and find solutions to unexplored problems. For example, if everyone around you is complaining about relationship problems, as a creative entrepreneur, think about how you can solve these problems and how your solution can lead to profits. Unlocking your brilliance in this example could be providing an anonymous blog in which couples can get help from professionals and other couples with similar experiences. Another idea could be starting a podcast series to talk about relationship problems. Brilliant ideas can unfold when you choose to solve rather than ignore life's challenges.

Risk-Taking: The difference between an idea and a product or service is the concept of risk. The human mind is capable of having many ideas. It can move from a current state to a desired result instantly. The problem is not in conceiving an idea but in going all the way to finding the needed solution. Entrepreneurs are some of the most famous risk takers. Let's say Anne has a wonderful idea to start an organic skin care line. The act of coming up with the concept does not define her as a brilliant entrepreneur. However, if she decides tomorrow to start her research, speak to business owners in the cosmetic industry, make a business plan, and raise funds she would be on her way to unlocking her brilliance within entrepreneurship. The next time you see a problem that needs fixing around you, will you look away or take the risk in solving it?

Resource Control: Successful entrepreneurs never take time for granted. They are keen enough to manage their time by planning out their schedules, giving themselves the opportunity to manage this scarce resource. Money is another resource that can be scarce. Knowing the best and most effective ways to manage this precious resource is a major skill that every entrepreneur must have. The management of resources for maximum profitability is not just about using the resources we want, but also about using them to achieve a greater return on our investment. Entrepreneurs must also develop their relationship skills with other people in order to build a good reputation and strong company image. You will unlock your brilliance by managing available resources such as time, money and people. Your emotions, judgment, reasoning, and communication will all contribute to your entrepreneurial success.

Discovering Your Weakness: The key to unlocking your brilliance may lie within discovering your weakness. The only way to do this is by stepping outside the bounds of your comfort zone or what I call your bear cave, the place that gives you warmth, safety, and protection. Your predictable space of retreat. Just as life requires different skills of survival, so does creative entrepreneurship.

Focus: The ability to focus is a strong sign of inner control and mental brilliance. How well do you focus? Knowing your level of concentration and how well you deal with distractions can help you rate your focus level. The goal of focus as a creative entrepreneur is to have total control over our time and resources. Nobody wants to do business with individuals who are always late and never meet deadlines.

~

We all have the capacity to unlock our inner brilliance. The five practices above will help speed up that process and maintain our growth to achieve our entrepreneurial goals. By seeking to uncover, polish, and improve on our personal attributes, we also are choosing a brighter path for our creative endeavors. Every creative entrepreneur that I have ever met throughout the course of my life has shared the goal of using their gifts to change the world for the better.

W.O.W

It's not for everyone but you will know if it's meant for you.

CHAPTER TEN

The sooner we unlock our superpowers,
the more battles we can win.

SUPERMAN VERSUS WONDER WOMAN

I grew up watching traditional superheroes on television such as Superman and Wonder Woman. As a kid, I truly believed that I could do all the cool things that Wonder Woman could do. I would even jump off the furniture in an attempt to fly. I fought off the invisible bullets with my make-believe bullet-proof bracelets and used my magic lasso to wrangle my villains. I see the close similarities between superheroes and entrepreneurs. Creative entrepreneurs choose to use their unique gifts to improve the world around them. They have a higher level of willingness to self-sacrifice compared to the general population. Some even believe that they can fly! Well, at least in terms of reaching the highest heights of success in their businesses.

Let's figure out how to spot if you are a superhero (or, in other words, a creative entrepreneur). Signs include the ability to tap into your intellectual skills and combine them with groundbreaking ideas that fulfill an existing need. You can intuitively turn your most novel thoughts into a creative venture or a product that others would pay for. On the flip side, like superheroes in disguise, you may be misunderstood, overlooked, or even criticized for your genius. Before volunteering to be the next entrepreneur to save the world, see if you check any of these boxes:

- Having the right energy level for the work required
- Good character and judgment
- The ability to think outside the box
- Business acumen
- The desire to expand your insight through courses and books
- Awareness to seek help to guide you through your business venture

With a deep desire to bring outstanding things into the world, creatives have to also analyze their qualifications for this unique role in society. I have listed these qualifications below for review. Do you embody these traits? If you are lacking in any and still have a desire to accept the challenge of creative entrepreneurship, commit to developing the areas you may fall short in.

THE SIX "ARE YOUS?"

Are You . . . Eager?: Exceedingly imaginative persons are extremely optimistic. No matter how insurmountable the obstacle, they choose to never give up. Their confidence and enthusiasm are enough to get them powered up over any cause or mission. They are especially skilled at hiding their exhaustion when working endlessly to complete a project or goal. Oftentimes this eagerness is transformed into singing or dancing while working. This is no surprise to other creatives, as this energy originates from being incredibly open and excited for what's to come. They do not follow the norm because their unique viewpoint is what powers their strength and enhances their distinct abilities. Highly creative entrepreneurs approach each new situation with the attitude of being an "apprentice," regardless of how mastered they already are.

Are You . . . Innovative?: Creative entrepreneurs are doers. They see the world as a beautiful place with endless opportunities worth exploring. They are known for putting in their very best until they have exhausted all of their imaginative energy trying to complete a task. These specialists and researchers flourish in the space of the obscure.

Are You . . . Inquisitive?: Creative entrepreneurs are not shy about pursuing their interests. They like to seek out and adapt to new things, and they appreciate the rush that comes with extraordinary discoveries. This is called the "genius bliss." This openness expands their likelihood of accomplishing something imaginative, while encouraging them to find even more profound experiences in their lives.

Are You . . . Unconventional?: Creative entrepreneurs are imaginative prodigies. They are exceptional, sincerely extraordinary, and energetic, which enables them to submerge themselves completely in their work. Have you ever wondered why certain artistic performances get a standing ovation by their audience, or why people still listen to classical music by our earliest composers? This is because these creatives were able to deliver a level of excellence that is not common and difficult to recreate.

Are You . . . a Visionary?: Creative entrepreneurs are dreamers with a passionate drive to see their vision and aspirations become a reality. Daydreaming enables imaginative individuals to focus on a future world with their creations. They are able to solve problems within the far-off travels of their imagination. Their gifts allow them to see how they can make a positive impact on the world. Their primary motivation is not material possessions but making life worth living, and finding a way to make a positive and lasting impact.

Are You . . . Adaptable?: Creative entrepreneurs are very flexible and can adapt to any environment they find themselves in. They love to explore new territories and are never afraid to take risks or try out something new. A true measurement of a creative entrepreneur is their rate of success in completing their objectives in entirely new environments. The gift to adapt to any environment makes the creative entrepreneur more resilient and capable of tackling any form of fear or failure.

> "The worst enemy to creativity is self-doubt."
> —Sylvia Plath

HOW TO UNLEASH YOUR SUPERNOVA

There are two types of businesspeople: the ones that can take their thoughts and monetize them, and the incredible ones that reexamine the future with their thoughts. Those that choose to change the future and dare to think differently can come up with the unimaginable. They take conviction-based action; they speculate around genuine and proposed ideas. They recreate the future by improving the present. They see things differently and set an example that inspires others to follow. They focus on new ways to make life simpler, less expensive, and increasingly enjoyable.

Extraordinary business ideas are already within you. With an open mind and strong purpose, you can easily tap into them. The first step in actualizing a groundbreaking idea is to relax, rest, and unwind. Next, be mindful of what is going on around you, perceive each moment as an opportunity to spark your supernova. Keep a journal or notepad with you to jot down anything fascinating or abnormal that you experience throughout the day. Change your mindset from following a repetitive routine to constantly seeking out new opportunities. Your ever-changing environment will make your brain continuously gauge the pros and cons of certain situations. Then, make a point of keeping up with business and political trends and industry news. In each of these areas, try thinking of solutions or business ideas. By doing all of the above-mentioned actions, you will be blown away by the overwhelming number of concepts you will come up with.

Finally, take advantage of the people you encounter each day by asking them what they think can be improved upon. When exploring this activity, focus on a specific target market, further develop the idea, and follow through with executing a plan. Here are some points to guide you in unleashing your supernova:

Begin with family: Consulting with family for incredible business ideas may be a good first step. Some family members can give you great ideas that can spur you to become even more creative as an entrepreneur. As part of your action plan, try building good relationships with some insightful family members, you never know what seeds they will help you plant and grow. Additionally, family will be the first to offer you monetary support to bring your concept to fruition. They know and trust you and helping you will only bring them joy.

Keep a list of the things that bug you: When you think about all of the things that bug you, the odds are that those same things probably also bug others. Keep a list of those things and spend time thinking of ways to improve them. Regularly adding to a diary, journal, or notebook is incredible for keeping track of those thoughts. It's an extraordinary method to structure and develop your ideas. What gets you irritated could be the next big business idea that will impact the world.

Turn your interests into a business: Your interests in life can help you find your business niche. Successful entrepreneurs around the world have taken their interest and turned it into a business empire. Your areas of interest can open doors for you when taken seriously, so why not start making a vigilant effort to explore them and maximize your potential?

Travel: Traveling can open your eyes to plenty of potential business ideas by reinvigorating your mind, body and soul. Visiting another place in the world is an extraordinary opportunity to meet new individuals, learn about different cultures, and invest time and energy touring. Such encounters can open your mind to better approaches for offering value as a creative entrepreneur.

Keep your eyes open: Recognizing present gaps in the marketplace is a clever method to come up with the most lucrative entrepreneurial ideas. Ask yourself, how can I increase the value of a current item? Where others see difficulties, you as a creative entrepreneur should see opportunities to deliver creative solutions. Concentrate on what you need to do to make a profitable business and keep your eyes open to market trends.

Relax and reflect: It can be difficult to think of incredible business ideas when your brain is packed with worry and anxiety throughout the day. Try to become more relaxed and reflective. Meditation and observation support unique thoughts that already exist within you and just need a little quiet time to reveal themselves.

Go online: Surfing the web can be a fun way to discover business solutions. Look into enterprise and industry-related networks, follow the trends, and stay updated on current events around the world. Web surfing can be an extraordinary means to great ideas but can also be a brain drain if it turns into a distraction. Explore the comment sections of reputable sites. Sometimes a complete stranger's inquiry can spark your next invention.

Meet new individuals: Working with experts in your field can greatly benefit your business. However, when you're surrounded by the same individuals all the time, your mind can become stagnant. Listening to the views of new people will allow your creativity to expand and expose you to new ideas.

Do your research: Is your idea feasible? Do your homework and prepare for any circumstance. Know the ins and outs of your market, where to get your resources, how to control them, as well as the laws and regulations concerning your business. Researching your idea can give you the confidence you need to begin an adventurous journey as an entrepreneur. The more you read about subjects concerning your business, the more successful you will be when actualizing your plans.

W.O.W

Preparation is the key to success.

CHAPTER ELEVEN

We are all creative beings by design.

~

HOW TO BOOST CREATIVITY

We are all creative. Whether we are painting or driving a garbage truck, we all have the ability to be inventive, strategic, think differently, solve problems, and help others. No matter what form it shows up in, know that you have some within you. Not only do you have the ability to be creative, but you can increase that level of creativity at any time.

As children, we were allowed to play and encouraged to use our imagination, but as adults, we are discouraged from playing and encouraged to work harder. As entrepreneurs, we have to play more and challenge ourselves to be inventive in as many situations as possible to strategize and improve. The more enjoyment you can get out of your day-to-day activities and the more fun you can build into your environment, the more productive you will be and the more prosperous your business will become.

Let's pretend that we are starting kindergarten all over again. You take naps in the middle of the day, your mom packed your favorite lunch, and you get to take recess outside where you run around with your best friends and then do fun projects like paint, build things, sing, dance, or learn about cool cultures around the world. Now, let's come back to the present moment. If you could turn your business into the coolest kindergarten experience, what would your day look like? Remember, building a business or becoming an entrepreneur doesn't mean all work and no play. Actually, it is just the opposite. The most successful creative entrepreneurs view their work as fun, surround themselves by their favorite people, eat well, and take time to rest and explore their creativity, be it through music, art, games, or physical movement. All of these activities help break the monotony, relieve anxiety, avoid fatigue, and stimulate new ideas.

Creativity is similar to a muscle that must be stretched, tested, and continuously pushed past its normal range of familiarity. There will be moments when you are not able to think of creative ideas as a result of stress or being too mentally or physically occupied. When this happens, attempting to tackle an issue and come up with a reasonable solution will seem very difficult. To help break out of this rut, find a leisure activity such as playing an instrument, chess, or running to help you unwind while giving your imagination a lift. Stepping away from your daily routine and doing something you haven't tried in a long time will keep your mind open to creative ideas.

Another surefire way to boost your creativity is to use other industries as your source of inspiration. For instance, if you are a blogger that gives relationship advice, take a look at other industries like finance, health, psychology and more. Find ways to weave these topics into your articles or perhaps tap into a new readership by offering relationship advice to other industry professionals.

Some of the best ideas come to us when we are not wracking our brains trying to force them out. I get great ideas right after a hot shower or while running or walking outside. Just giving our minds a rest can be all we need to get that extra kick of creativity. Need more ideas? No problem. Take a look at the creativity-boosting tricks below:

Get social: Head out to a movie and shut your brain down from labor for a couple of hours. Call a friend or family member to help alleviate the pressure that is blocking you from finding the level of creativity you are searching for. Investing time with your family is probably going to lessen your feelings of anxiety and provide you with more energy to put toward creative thinking.

Request help: Requesting help is not a sign of weakness. Getting advice from the people that you trust and respect is a smart thing to do. Learning from the experiences of others can positively impact your life and business.

Remember good memories: Recalling good times and victories of the past will make it a lot simpler for you to find creative motivation.

Revisit your values: We model our environment to reflect our core values. Reminding ourselves of those values can motivate us to achieve our goals.

Tame the perfectionist: Perfectionism can cause you to chip away at or ruin your best work. Try not to obsess over getting everything right. When an idea comes to you, act on it and figure out the bumps along the way.

Read biographies of creative people: A great way to invigorate your mind is to read stories about successful creative entrepreneurs. You can learn a lot just by finding out about what worked for these great personalities and how they overcame hurdles on the road to success. Be open to learn from both their triumphs and disappointments.

Know your goals: Thoroughly consider your long-term targets and organize them into shorter-term action plans. Smaller milestones may stimulate strategies more easily than the bigger, more stressful goals.

Write: Writing about your daily activities can capture some profound thoughts. You can also draw something if you do not feel like writing; this can also help you get your creative juices flowing.

Enjoy the gift of nature: Go outside and breathe in some fresh air, enjoy the birds, flower gardens, and other natural scenes. Nature can inspire you in more ways than you can imagine.

Work out: Exercising your physical body can inspire new, imaginative designs.

Get a massage: Massages can help calm the body, making it simpler to find solutions to problems and think of new ideas.

Play a game: Games can help stimulate creative thoughts. Go to an arcade and play video games, or perhaps take out your favorite board game or deck of cards. The point is to find time to play games you really like to inspire fun and creativity.

Get some rest: Try not to worry about fame. It is alright if your work is not well-known at the moment. Overworking due to the pressure of delivering something exceptional from the very beginning can really make it hard to put anything out to the public. To avoid brain blocks, take the necessary time to rest when you are feeling exhausted.

Get a creative space: Carve out an exclusive space that you retreat to when you need to be inventive. You can do this by finding a corner in your house that is free from any form of distraction. Once you discover your creative spot, go there frequently and notice how easily your innovative thoughts come to you.

> "To be creative means to be in love with life. You can be creative only if you love life enough that you want to enhance its beauty, you want to bring a little more music to it, a little more poetry to it, a little more dance to it."
> —Osho

HOW TO GENERATE IDEAS AS A CREATIVE ENTREPRENEUR

Incredible ideas can spring up surprisingly when there is motivation present. One of the ways I motivated myself recently is by signing up for an improv class. If you have never taken one before, improvisation is a form of live theater in which the performers make up the scene in the moment and use elements inspired by the audience. When I signed up for the course, I had no idea what I was getting myself into.

As a newbie to live theater, I was hungry to learn more. During the class, we had to act out scenes with complete strangers—with no script. (Talk about pressure!) It was a huge learning experience for me and one of the best ways to boost my creativity. I think every entrepreneur would benefit from taking an improv class to develop the tools needed to generate creativity on the spot.

When doing improv, one of the most important skills is your ability to listen. If you are too far ahead in thought or dwelling on what you did or didn't say a few moments ago, you are going to miss your cue for the scene. However, to properly listen, you have to be fully present to the scene unfolding in front of you. There is a certain peace and calm when you are actively in the moment. Words, descriptions, and solutions to the imagined problems being played out just magically appear. Another important skill in improv is the willingness to be in total agreement with the statements your co-stars share with you. For example, if they say that we are all on a rocket ship right now heading to Mars, you have to follow with conversation and developments that completely support that idea. Now, remember, it's not about the idea, it's about completely believing in the idea, no matter how inconceivable it appears to be. Let's recap. The critical skills needed to begin successfully improving are:

- Listening
- Being present
- Believing in the idea
- Supporting the idea in words and action

Do you see where I am going with this? If you likened being an entrepreneur to being an improv actor, learning your business as if you were learning to successfully improv would only guarantee you many victories and lots of laughs along the way. Beyond enrolling in an upcoming improv class, below are some additional methods for stimulating your imagination:

Selection: Pick the idea that you feel will work best for your target audience. The best idea isn't always the first one you come up with or the one you love the most but the one that is backed by your research, maintains your interests, and fills a strong need for your clients.

Mind mapping: A mind map is a diagram used to visualize links between different concepts. Every possibility or thought is recorded on paper and the connections are made between those concepts to help new concepts form.

Storyboarding: A storyboard is a visual story used to clarify or investigate ideas. Storyboards enable creative entrepreneurs to lay out the data discovered in their research. Pictures, feedback, and other data are placed on a physical board to help further develop the understanding and connections between different ideas.

Role-playing: This imaginary system of visualizing what it's like to be in someone else's shoes is not only fun but can also help creative entrepreneurs let their guard down and see solutions from a different perspective.

Thought challenging: Thought challenging is an exercise in which several answers to a question are objectively explored. The purpose of a thought challenge is to enable you to shape and direct that question at a particular crowd to get new thoughts and one-of-a-kind bits of knowledge.

W.O.W

Once you find your well, you will never be thirsty for ideas.

CHAPTER TWELVE

Never tell an athlete it can't be done.
Become your coach.
Train your inner athlete.

AWAKEN YOUR INNER ATHLETE

Athletes need to train consistently and at the highest level to maintain their optimal performance. They also need the right mindset to endure the training, length of time, injuries, setbacks, or naysayers along the way. Even with natural talent, without the proper guidance, vision, and dedication, athletes can easily fail unless they are committed for the long haul and decisive in never taking their eye off the prize.

As a creative entrepreneur, you need to channel your inner athlete and adopt the mindset of a champion. Surround yourself with the right people, influences, inspiration, and seek out the proper training for your skill level to sustain the long haul ahead. The path to entrepreneurship is not easy and definitely not for everyone, but a successful brand will always have an owner, so why shouldn't it be you?

As with sports, every year brings new contenders and winners, so don't ever become complacent in your positioning. Stay alert and continuously seek ways to re-invent yourself to stay ahead of the competition. See your business as a game, learn the rules, and play to win.

> "Don't think. Thinking is the enemy of creativity. It's self-conscious and anything self-conscious is lousy. You can't 'try' to do things. You simply 'must' do things."
> —Ray Bradbury

Persistence is a key factor for long-term success. Understanding from the beginning that everything usually takes longer than anticipated can help this process along. Don't let disappointment sway your choice of becoming an entrepreneur. Many brilliant individuals never succeed, not because they didn't have a good product or know their target audience, but because they gave up too soon. Just imagine, what if Michael Jordan gave up basketball in high school because he thought that he didn't have what it took to be a pro player? Not only did he make it to the NBA despite a rocky start in the sport, he became one of the best players of all time.

The world is brimming with "could have been" individuals who have awesome thoughts and goals but did not have the stamina to keep going. A considerable lot of them gave up too quickly because the road ahead appeared excessively hard, overwhelming, or frightening. Basically, they were not mentally or physically prepared to take the necessary steps to succeed. The depressing truth is, if you are not willing to accomplish your dreams, another person will be. Someone else will pick up where you left off and succeed where you surrendered. Only the brave and strong get the chance to see their labor become a true reality. The distinction between the individuals who triumph and those who do not is the capacity to keep working tirelessly, long after the rest have dropped out. Persistence is easy when things are going well, but harder and even more important is it to persist when things are not going according to plan.

Persistence carries you through the difficult times and unpredictable downturns. It gives you self-control in the most trying moments. It tugs at you to keep trotting along regardless of setbacks or insurmountable obstacles. I love the story of Mary Lou Retton, the first American female gymnast to win the all-around Olympic gold medal. About five weeks before the Olympic games, Mary Lou suffered a knee injury after performing at a local gym. Recovering from her surgery just in time, she went on to become a legacy and inspiration for generations to follow as she claimed the top spot for the all-around. Mary Lou Retton had plenty of reasons to give up and throw in the towel when her dream seemed to have eluded her. Instead, she pushed forward and performed to the very best of her ability. That is all she could do and that is all any of us can do. We just need to keep showing up. Here are some other steps you can take to awaken your inner entrepreneurial athlete.

1. **Conquer failures**: When entrepreneurs pitch a new business and strike out, they need to learn from every failure and embrace the uncertainty that coincides with having a creative venture. Experiencing failures as an entrepreneur is unavoidable but overcoming your fears and failures in business will help you stay optimistic and open to more opportunities.

2. **Challenge yourself**: Triumphs help build self-confidence and motivation, but only when you challenge yourself to reach for the highest peak in whatever you do. Discover the harmony between your longing to succeed and your inclination to challenge the status quo. If you need to test yourself, take on activities without the help of others. Defining growth objectives for yourself is an extraordinary method to add some adventure into your workday and improve your talent and aptitude. Setting records and breaking them will only motivate you to grow as a creative entrepreneur.

3. **Take risks**: Never let the fear of failure stop you from achieving your goals. Success comes to the brave who dare to take risks and never give up. Nobody can get away from the internal voice telling them they can't do something, who gives an alert at each advancement and offers doubt at every chance. However, you can figure out how to identify with and accept it for what it is. Your inner voice absolutely does not have the right to hold you back nor the ability to stop you from becoming the dominant focal point in your own life. Regardless of whether you will choose to turn into a businessperson or ascend in the positions you hold at your organization, you need to make bold moves even when you are frightened and develop the capacity to go forward despite mishaps or setbacks. When you do, you will discover the strength and assuredness that you have. It takes gigantic measures of fearlessness to overcome the fear of disappointment. The athletic entrepreneur is not easily discouraged; you will get better with time. You must be very resilient to follow through every step in your business endeavor.

4. **Be truthful**: Aim to be open and honest in all your business dealings. Never try to portray who or what you are not, as

untruths can quickly ruin your reputation or tarnish your brand. At all times, be upfront with everybody around you, including yourself. Practice being as transparent as possible and do not intentionally mislead people. Successful entrepreneurs understand that they must be straightforward with themselves and keep their partners and investors in the know about the financial and general state of the business, including any difficulties they are experiencing. When you are consistently honest with yourself and others, you enable your uniqueness to radiate through while remaining thoughtful, true, receptive and reasonable. Figuring out how to be truthful is about straightforwardness, and the challenge is to do this even when the reality of circumstances is hard to swallow. Never be afraid to speak the truth no matter the consequences. Good legacies are built over the years by maintaining a good reputation.

W.O.W

You can deny the desire but never the signs to achieve the desire.

CHAPTER THIRTEEN

The trick is to always see the light,
never the tunnel.

~

THE SURVIVAL GAME

Consider the story of how LEGO founder Ole Kirk Christiansen developed the survival instinct to revamp his business after so many downfalls. Christiansen survived the Great Recession, the loss of his wife, and raising his four children alone. Not long after he founded LEGO, a fire broke out at the workshop, destroying every one of his illustrations and models. Two other significant workshop fires occurred after that, and revenue stopped coming in, but Christiansen overcame these difficulties and found the strength to reconstruct his workshop every time. Because Christiansen never gave up, the world is blessed with LEGO's incredible source of creative energy and motivation, which continue to positively affect both kids and grown-ups today. Here are the skills you'll need to survive the rise and fall of entrepreneurship.

1. **Aspiration:** To be an entrepreneur you must first aspire to achieve no matter what business you choose to build. It is this aspiration that keeps you in check when depression or failure comes. Survival throughout everyday life and in business has always been about the human voyage. Never give up—keep aspiring to make the world a better place.

2. **Willingness to learn:** In order to survive the game of entrepreneurship, it is important to regularly research the best individuals in your industry. Never be reluctant to request their expertise or leverage their connections. Leaders are learners; they stay ahead because they realize that learning helps them make the right forecast and analysis with greater success. Attend seminars, subscribe to webinars, follow great mentors across your social media platforms, and make sure you are always learning as an entrepreneur.

3. **Capacity to listen:** To be a successful entrepreneur you need to be a good listener. You do not want to be labeled as a boss who nobody wants to talk to because you are very temperamental and easy to anger. This can make you lose talented staff and good customers. Communication is a two-way street. Focus on others' inspirations and interests, and from there, the sky is the limit. Let your capacity to listen give you insights to perform better.

4. **Selling ability:** Success in entrepreneurship stems from selling yourself, as reflected in your online brand as well as the popularity, impact, and trust you earn from friends, clients, bosses, and the overall population. If you desire to make a name for yourself in your industry, build a solid personal brand and focus on making sure that those around you are clear about your business objectives.

5. **Work ethic:** Being an entrepreneur could bring you fame and status. Be that as it may, a great deal of diligence, hard work, and extended periods of time are required to launch something new. To be effective, you must execute and always keep your word. Be true to your customers and remember that every detail matters. Always know where you stand in your business niche and how you compare to your competitors. To stay in business, make it a priority to be known for your positive attributes. For instance, a fashion designer who sells dresses online and delivers poorly constructed products would quickly develop a bad reputation. This alone can cause other prospective clients not to purchase from that fashion designer. Strong work ethic is good for business; use it as a guide to stay true to your principles in all your business affairs.

6. **Structure:** Structure helps entrepreneurs run a more effective business; they do not need to head all departments of their company to avoid making wrong decisions. A well-organized infrastructure guides the decision-making process and helps in the accountability of business operations.

7. **Financial control:** Realizing how to oversee and develop your accounts is vital to business success. Inability to oversee funds opens you to the danger of becoming unsustainable, which can bring an end to your business. Put systems in place to create financial control and judiciousness. Life is a lot simpler when you have great budgetary skills or add someone to your team that does. If you haven't already, begin tracking your purchasing habits to find places where you might be accidentally overspending. Save your receipts and record your buys in a worksheet or database, arranging them so you can easily recognize areas where you can make improvements. If

needed, educate yourself on both useful and specialized processes that will enable you to build your salary and reallocate resources to keep your business pushing forward.

8. **Influential writing:** Invest in ways to showcase strong written communication to increase your chances of being heard and your product or company being seen. These communication outlets should include emails, blog posts, and published articles showcasing your areas of expertise.

9. **Relationship building:** In our current economy, you need a strong network to gain ground. From referrals to advice, your circle of contacts is your most profitable asset. Network, network, network and watch opportunities come your way and doors easily open as you pursue your dreams.

10. **Stress management:** Regardless of how you do it, be it through staying organized, changing your attitude, or prayer and meditation, make it a priority to keep stress in check. Achieving this goal keeps both your business and your well-being in amazing condition.

W.O.W

A long-term mindset takes discipline.

CHAPTER FOURTEEN

Create ideas with the speed of the hare,
and the faith of the turtle.

~

YOUR ARMOR AND YOUR AX

Actors must develop a thick skin and accept that rejection is a part of the business, but it only takes one yes for the right role to propel them to the furthest heights of stardom. Similarly, creative entrepreneurs must be open to accepting failure and what comes with the process of recovering from it. You must be flexible, open-minded, and curious. If you possess these qualities, then the mistakes become reset buttons, and the disappointments become a means of building up your armor and sharpening your ax. The stars will eventually align if you stay the course, and the time will present itself for your dreams to come true. Do you have the patience, vision, and courage to see it through?

~

> "Human resources are like natural resources; they're often buried deep. You have to go looking for them, they're not just lying around on the surface. You have to create the circumstances where they show themselves."
> —Ken Robinson

Once you establish an attainable way to propel yourself forward toward reaching your goals, become very intentional about securing startup capital, surrounding yourself with extraordinary people, and getting the word out about your vision. When you start to make profits, reinvest wisely for better returns, develop an in-depth knowledge of every intricate detail of your business, and apply the strategies that move you closer to prosperity. Most importantly, keep following your dreams. Follow these steps to help you on your way to entrepreneurial success:

1. **Kill fear:** To be successful in entrepreneurship, you must immediately make a move to eliminate fear when you see it coming, because the business world is full of great uncertainties. Discover approaches to lessen and deal with your fears so that you can be more prosperous in your business. All businesspeople make mistakes along the way to progress so don't let failure be your excuse for inaction. Look at mistakes as a time for learning and assume full responsibility when they occur. It's not the mistake that matters but how you handle or recover from it. No one remembers the runner that fell, just the one that got back up and crossed the finish line. Success is not for the faint at heart; it is for the strong-willed entrepreneur.

2. **Find a mentor:** Finding a mentor is an incredible method to become more familiar with your industry. Experienced

mentors can teach not only great business lessons but also how to have the right mindset to succeed. They can be your cheerleader when you need one most to empower you not to give up when you are at your lowest moments.

3. **Make a plan:** Before beginning any business, planning is essential. Structure your company accordingly, carry out a feasibility report, and develop a business plan supported by strong financial forecasts to run a successful venture. When you have gathered all the necessary data, set a date and time you wish to begin. This timeline should also act as guide for obtaining necessary starting capital. Planning is an effective way to reach your milestones.

4. **Remain eager:** You need positive energy to accelerate success. Always strive to be an inspiration. Be the light that shines brighter and never goes dim. Be eager and full of ambition and never let go of your dreams—this is the secret to success.

5. **Work smart:** Diligent work is a vital component to prevailing as an entrepreneur; however, workaholic behavior prompts weakness, which prompts mistakes. Entrepreneurs need to figure out how to brilliantly and effectively achieve more from their business without falling into the trap of overworking.

6. **Maintain relationships:** Business connections matter. Quite often organizations will like to work with other organizations they like and trust. Your capacity to relate with businesspeople inside your industry will be very beneficial to you. Business connections have a way of helping you get referrals, recommendations, bigger contracts, and good business partners. By sustaining associations with staff, banks,

government agencies, consultants, suppliers, clients, lawyers, investors, friends, and family you can set the wheels in motion to make sure your business is always up and running. To become a successful entrepreneur, keep your business relationships solid.

7. **Stay informed:** Keep your eyes open to industry trends. There are numerous open doors emerging in the business world every day. Attend seminars, workshops, listen to the news, know your competitors, your market, the exchange rate, and what regulations or policies your government is coming up with. Always be informed, never be caught unaware.

8. **Find the right business:** Start with a business that you love very much. Pick a field that you are passionate about. A business enterprise is arduous work, so you need to concentrate on something you care about. This is a proven way to stay motivated in trying times.

9. **Trust your instincts:** Entrepreneurs are often guilty of being married to their spreadsheets and business plans. However, your intuition and heart are your absolute best guides for basic leadership. Although data is helpful, nobody knows as much about you and your vision as you do. Don't underestimate the power and knowing of your inner voice.

10. **Dismiss the inner workaholic:** Although hard work is a critical component to an accomplished creative entrepreneur, workaholic behavior can lead to exhaustion and missteps. Recognizing our greatest skills early and finding ways to take care of the areas we are not strong in will save us a lot of time and money in the long run. Being productive and working

more efficiently is the ultimate objective, not just working longer or harder.

11. **Outsource:** Hire individuals to do the things you are bad at or having trouble executing due to time constraints or limited resources. This will enable you to concentrate on the aspects of your business that you excel at. If you are overwhelmed with the thought of additional staff or infrastructure, take advantage of the gig economy and hire from the vast array of specialists, freelancers, and contractors.

12. **Wake up energized:** Those that start their day with great zeal show the most resilience in pushing through the most difficult of circumstances.

13. **Be decisive:** You must be quick to make choices. Hesitation can lead to missed opportunities, lack of morale among your team, and an erosion of your own self-confidence. Learn to trust the decisions you make and accept the results, good or bad.

14. **Assume responsibility:** Whenever something is not right, never be reluctant to confront it. The sooner you accept the error, the quicker you can figure out how to resolve it and move past it. An attitude of accountability will help you get back on your feet sooner every time.

15. **Spot the value in your product:** The product or service that you offer must have something exceptional about it to catch the attention of consumers. Give your clients the best product that suits their needs and they in turn will continuously come back to you.

16. **Sell your idea:** Your role as an entrepreneur is to persuade individuals that whatever you are selling is the best choice available to them. Get focused around developing the messaging that sets your product apart from the rest.

W.O.W

Once you figure out that life is a game, you have won.

CHAPTER FIFTEEN

Love the beauty of the caterpillar,
as if it already looks like a butterfly.

~

WHEN IN DOUBT, CHOOSE BLUE

When it comes to targeting clients or markets, take a blue ocean approach. As a visual person, this helps me a lot in deciding between products, services, and customers that I want to target. Visualize a shark attacking a school of fish. If you are a lone fish, separated from the crowd, you will have the highest chance of survival because the shark will feast where there is a greater number of fish. When developing your business plan for execution, give it the blue ocean quiz to see if it has a greater chance of survival.

THE BLUE OCEAN QUIZ

1. **Is there a space in the ocean where you can live all by yourself or next to no more than one or two existing fish?**

What does the competitive landscape look like? Are you the first in the marketplace, the second, or the third? If you are not one of the top three, revisit your idea or the market.

2. **Is there enough food to survive?** Are there enough people that have this problem or that will buy your proposed solution to support a business? Does your product market have growth potential?

3. **Will you be alone for a while or is a fast approaching pool of fish close behind?** Do you see your current idea being imitated by someone else? If so, come up with a variation of the idea so you can remain the only fish for miles. You want to give yourself enough time to develop and test your business model before your competitors approach. A bigger company with more resources can more easily launch a similar solution and immediately squeeze you from the market, so take the time to find the right positioning to ensure your company long-term success.

> "Be brave enough to live creatively. The creative is the place where no one else has ever been. You have to leave the city of your comfort and go into the wilderness of your intuition. You cannot get there by bus, only by hard work, risking, and by not quite knowing what you are doing. What you will discover will be wonderful: Yourself."
>
> —Alan Alda

Once you find, attract, and grow your customer base, there will be less worry regarding your competitors. Offering exceptional products and customer service will make it hard for other businesses to compete. Below are great places to start when developing your strategy around customer acquisition and success.

1. **Find your target audience**: Study the statistics in your industry and those of your competitors. This will help you find a target audience that no one is currently reaching.

2. **Offer incentives**: Think of possible ways you can scale your business to build your customer base. Offer incentives to keep your customers satisfied and coming back.

3. **Create additional products**: Bring in more customers by creating additional products alongside your core products. For instance, a publishing house could offer branded baseball caps, T-shirts, etc. while pursuing the core business of publishing books. Offering a wider variety of products allows for more opportunity to grow your customer base.

4. **Enter international markets**: Taking your product to a global market could be a great way to rapidly grow your venture. Selling through Amazon has proven to be a cost-effective platform for entrepreneurs to market their products to customers around the world.

5. **Online classes**: Becoming an instructor is an extraordinary avenue of advancing your online presence and market reach. The online class is a great opportunity for a creative entrepreneur to grow naturally and attain a certain level of fame in their industry.

6. **Meet customer needs**: Even if you create a product that initially fulfills the consumer's needs, eventually they will want more. This is where customer reviews and opinions come in.

When you request both, you can get inside the heads of your customers and find out exactly what their needs are. Find out how they want your product to improve and grow, and as a result they will grow alongside you.

7. **Improve customer service**: Having the best customer service experience gives your business a good brand image, which is a great way to gain customer loyalty. Make your customers feel unique and special by expressing your appreciation. When they have questions or complaints, set aside some time to address them. When you treat customers well, they may even refer your business to others.

8. **Digital marketing**: Take advantage of all social media platforms and learn how to leverage each of their advantages. Ensure your business is well situated online as digital marketing is now the standard way to introduce your business to potential clients, increase traffic to your site, and take your product to people across the world. Watch for industry trends in order to have the best content strategy that will maximize the sale of your products or services.

9. **Host events**: Hosting online or in-person events is a great way to learn more about your customers. Grow brand loyalty and awareness by inviting your best clients to exclusive experiences to get to know them better.

10. **Give back**: Having a mindful ethos for your brand is a wonderful way to draw in new clients. They will trust you more if you are ethically and socially aware and will want to contribute to your platform. Your efforts will simultaneously help the community while creating a strong brand legacy.

11. **Guard the existing market**: When developing your business, you always want to attract new clients. However, the majority of your income will likely come from returning clients, so marketing to existing clients is often the most strategic way to expand your business.

12. **Request referrals**: One of the most effortless ways to expand your business is to ask for business referrals. If you ask your present clients to refer you to a friend that can benefit from your offerings, they likely will.

13. **Partake in trade shows**: Public exhibitions can be an incredible method to develop your client base. Try to choose the events that best align with your product and buyer.

14. **Grow**: Never become too complacent in where you are as customer needs are always changing. By staying tuned in, you can quickly adopt new ideas immediately to further develop your business.

15. **Keep detailed financial records**: Knowing where your business stands monetarily can help you confront and improve potential difficulties.

16. **Accept competition**: Rivalry breeds the best outcomes. Having others around you doing something similar and testing the waters of success can be a guidepost for you, especially if you are a newbie in your industry. Embrace your competition and observe what they are doing right. Adapt what you know works as it relates to improving cashflow. Continue to use your unique perspective and qualities to maintain your advantage.

17. **Be creative**: Continuously search for new approaches to improve your business and protect it from unforeseen challenges.

18. **Remain focused**: Don't be discouraged if your business doesn't scale right away or show immediate profits. Be patient and find other things to appreciate along the way. This will help you focus on your longer-term entrepreneurial success.

19. **Plan to make sacrifices**: The lead-up to beginning a business is diligent work, and even after you launch, the workload doesn't decrease. Knowing this ahead of time can help you plan your time between family, friends, and your business.

W.O.W

Learn to appreciate the journey because in the end, that is the only thing that matters.

CHAPTER SIXTEEN

*The truth lies in the present moment only,
nothing else.*

~

MINDFULNESS HACKS

What in the world does mindfulness have to do with creative entrepreneurship? Mindfulness helps us remember our "why." It also helps us appreciate all of the little accomplishments we make along the way. Many times, we get lost in our own hustle, and that hustle can quickly lead to a purposeless pursuit of things that have lost their meaning. By being mindful, we are reminded of the joys that each day brings. When we can find pleasure or happiness in the world around us, we contribute to our greatest inner brilliance.

The Merriam-Webster Dictionary defines mindfulness as "the practice of maintaining a nonjudgmental state of heightened or complete awareness *of one*'s thoughts, emotions, or experiences on a moment-to-moment basis." According to Zen Master, global political leader, poet, and activist Thich Nhat

Hanh, "Mindfulness shows us what is happening in our bodies, our emotions, our minds, and in the world. Through mindfulness, we avoid harming ourselves and others."

Many successful entrepreneurs such as Richard Branson and Bobby Axelrod practice mindfulness to balance their endless lists of emails, calls, and tasks. It helps them slow down the already supercharged work culture they have created for themselves. There are many ways to practice mindfulness, such as yoga and meditation, that allow us to better process information while managing stress.

John Kabat Zinn, founder of mindfulness-based stress reduction, claims that mindfulness is the act of paying attention in the present moment without judgment. As simple as this sounds, most individuals do not live in the present moment. Where are they? They are getting anxious about future events that have not yet occurred or worrying over past decisions or experiences. Life events such as parenthood, starting a business, or a major move can all cause some level of stress or throw us off our game. To help counter these roller-coaster moments, it is good to make balance a priority.

Not too long ago, I went through a very big cross-country move. Before relocating, I was deeply rooted in my tropical lifestyle. The decision to move, although a great opportunity, wasn't as appealing to me at first. Moving away from warm, sunny days, easy access to the ocean, and an active outdoor lifestyle was not the picture I was ready to paint. Instead, the idea of relocating out of state was a very jarring thought.

Once arriving at our new home, I spent weeks sulking over how much I missed my friends, old routine, and colorful surroundings. One day out of nowhere, the thought of meditating came to me. At our old home, I used to meditate daily for about forty-five minutes before going to bed. For some reason that went away, as did many of the routine activities I was once involved in. I slowly began to incorporate these activities back into my daily routine and was pleasantly surprised to find that such small actions brought balance and peace back into my life. They allowed me to stay in the present moment.

After taking a mindfulness course, I started putting the puzzle pieces together of how to be mindful in avoiding stress and creating balance in my life. Less stress equals more productivity and creativity. Without productivity and creativity, it is hard to bring any idea to fruition or push any project forward with great success. The mindfulness class was extremely enlightening. I found out how much I didn't know about mindfulness, and how to teach what I learned to others. I immediately incorporated the knowledge I gained into various aspects of my life. Below are cool discoveries I learned and found extremely useful. Challenge yourself to learn how you can implement mindfulness into your daily routine. You will only benefit from its proven effects.

1. **Switch up your meditation position**: You can meditate while walking and lying down. If you're like me, the typical seated position doesn't always feel comfortable.

2. **There are many forms of mindfulness**: Mindfulness exists in many forms of movement, such as walking, running, gardening, hiking, and taekwondo. Find a new state of peace and calm while enjoying these activities by paying more attention to your surroundings.

3. **Embodied learning**: The concept of receiving new information through the movement of the body is a form of being in the present moment. This is a strong component of most sports, which can explain why they are enjoyable to so many people.

4. **Heart rhythm meditation**: The connection between breathing and the heart plays a big role in our physical and mental health. This meditation's conscious breathing technique can help you push through especially challenging moments. (Every little bit helps when trying to finish that last set of squats!)

THE MELODY OF CREATIVITY

Want to bring attention to your thoughts, create awareness, and help minimize negative thinking? Well, sound may be an easy and effective tool to use. For thousands of years, sound has been known as a powerful means of increasing one's ability to be more mindful or aware. From the sweet singing of birds and the rhythmic flow of water to humming in the shower, sound can be that everlasting connection between one and the present moment. It can be a simple go-to answer for maintaining a positive state of mind.

For centuries, cultures from around the world have used sound as a form of healing from depression, anxiety, and stress. Tibetan singing bowls have a long history of being used in this way. These ancient instruments were made of metal and used by Tibetan monks to reduce stress and anxiety. Below are some modern-day recommendations for using sound to help improve workplace mindfulness.

1. **Place your workspace outside where nature is present or near an open window where you have a clear view of the outside and the ability to hear the sounds that come with it.** If you are unable to experience nature's sounds in real time, choose a nature sound of your choice from your favorite music app.

2. **Add music to your workspace.** Select music or sounds that soothe you such as the sound of Tibetan bowls, jazz, or classical music.

3. **Take work breaks to engage in an activity of embodied movement such as walking, tai chi, dancing, gardening, biking, or jogging while playing your favorite songs in the background.** The combined sensations will be sure to put you in a pleasant and uplifted mood.

4. **When done with your work for the day, take five to ten minutes to wind down to a calming instrumental while sitting or lying still.** This can be a melody of a certain frequency, such as 528 Hz, or a guided meditation to the same frequency.

> "All our knowledge has its origin in our perceptions."
> —Leonardo Da Vinci

WHAT'S THE HYPE AROUND 528 HZ?

Various tones have been used since ancient times to promote the health of our mind and body. These tones are called solfeggio frequencies, and 528 Hz is one of these frequencies. Dr. Joseph Puleo brought the six-tone scale of solfeggio frequencies back into awareness in the 1970s. It is believed that this six-tone scale brings the mind, body, and spirit into harmony by balancing our energies. It is known for its energizing and healing affects and is ideal to listen to if you want to relax or wind down.

Harvard-trained doctor Leonard Horowitz calls 528 Hz the universal healer. He noticed that 528 Hz is vital to everything known to mankind, which includes the air we breathe, the water we drink, the grass underneath our feet, and the sun's beams that shine overall. Its vibrations interface and resound with everything inside us and around us, on both a physical and non-physical level. I have personally experimented with 528 Hz and its effects on my sleep pattern, mood, etc. When I listen to it throughout the night, I wake up more easily. When I listen to it while working, it naturally brings me to a calmer state. I believe that as creatives, we must find novel ways to keep our minds in peace mode to produce our best work. Therefore, hacks like this one are invaluable to boost creativity and beat burnout.

CHAPTER SEVENTEEN

When there are bumps in the road,
the strongest car will always outlast
the fastest one.

~

OVERCOME BURNOUT AND BOREDOM

While interviewing Nzinga Blake, founder of Fashion Ambassadors, I asked her to name the three traits that she felt were most needed to pursue entrepreneurship. She replied by saying:

> Fearlessness, determination and faith—faith in yourself and/or in a higher power is paramount in becoming an entrepreneur. Fear often destroys our faith, which is why you have to be fearless. Once you can overcome your fear and have faith in yourself, you will be unstoppable! I always have to remind myself—if you don't believe in yourself, then why should others believe in you? Everyone should always work on knowing that they are deserving of success.

Consistent pressure makes entrepreneurs feel powerless, disappointed, and totally depleted which can lead to burnout, boredom, and loneliness. During your entrepreneurial journey you could get to a point where issues appear to be impossible, everything looks distressing, and it becomes too difficult to support yourself. The pitfalls in entrepreneurship can undermine your activity, your connections, and your well-being.

FAIL FEARLESSLY

Shortly after opening my showroom on 7th Avenue in New York City, I landed my first consulting client. Although I was not actively looking to become a consultant or advisor to creative founders, I quickly realized that this opportunity was the perfect marriage between my master's in clinical psychology and my fashion design skills. This first project was more design-based and I was asked to create a few samples that would then be sent to Oprah Winfrey as a gift. My client had a new fashion company and a close friend that could get her pieces directly to the queen of daytime television. My responsibilities included designing the line, finding the fabric, and overseeing the production of the garments. I was about eight months pregnant when this project presented itself, and that wasn't a deterrent for me accepting it, but I knew that eventually I would have to hand over some of the responsibility to my assistant.

Now, to set the stage on this scene, fabric selection happens to be my specialty. One of the reasons why people loved my designs was because of the unique fabrics I selected. Identifying the right fabric is one of the most important steps in creating a high-quality garment. With hesitation, I asked my assistant to handle this part of the project and then to ship the finished items off to the client. After a couple of weeks went by, I heard back from the client with feedback that Oprah was not impressed with the fabric choices. My heart sank when I heard this news because I could have hit that out of the park if I hadn't assigned the project to my less experienced assistant.

Deep down, I knew I was nervous about creating something for such a famous person. Delegating the one task that I knew I had exceptional skills in was risky and could have been avoided. Although I was further along in my pregnancy and couldn't as easily commute to and from the showroom, I could have arranged for the items to be shipped to me for quality control. Instead, I blindly approved the fabric selection, perhaps knowing that since I only was partially involved, I could only be partially blamed if the items were ultimately rejected. My own inexperience and lack of guidance cost me an opportunity of a lifetime. If my client's line was accepted with accolades, it could have meant instant fame for me as the young designer behind the collection. This experience showed me that a great concept alone is not enough. The quality of the product you are offering is what matters for initial acceptance. The irony is that quality and aesthetic were the very things I was known for as a rising designer and ultimately one of the very things I failed to deliver for that project. Thankfully, I took to heart the lessons learned that day and never repeated that mistake again. Additionally, I was fortunate to get a second chance when the same client hired me years later for an even bigger project.

I have personally experienced wanting something so badly that the image of you failing at it is too much to bear. To avoid the emotional collateral, sometimes you create a circumstance to guarantee failure, therefore removing the element of surprise. It is almost as if you are preparing yourself for the negative outcome because failing without preparation seems worse. Trust me, it doesn't feel any better if you are emotionally expecting to fail. If you are going after something you truly want, go big, because the best thing that can happen is that you succeed. At the end of the day, you deserve to receive all that you want in life!

So, how do you recover from failure? Take on a new motto. *Fail fearlessly.* If we see failure as a positive thing, we remove the anxiety that surrounds it. If we choose to see failure as a tool that helps us learn and grow, we can never lose in any situation. For example, a failed marriage can bring the broken couple to new, better matches. Therefore, did they fail at the first marriage or succeed at learning more about what they want out of a relationship? Failure can help you narrow down what works and what doesn't if you choose to pay attention and grow from each lesson.

BURNOUT IS REAL

Burnout is a response to drawn out or incessant stress and is portrayed by weariness, negativity, and sentiments of decreased proficiency. It happens when you feel overpowered, sincerely depleted, and unfit to satisfy consistent needs. The greater part of us have days when we feel powerless, overburdened, or undervalued while trying to stay strong. As the pressure builds, we may start to lose the intrigue and inspiration that drive our entrepreneurial aspirations.

In the end, you may feel like you don't have anything more to give if the negative impacts of burnout overflow into all aspects of your life. To counter burnout, having a feeling of direction is exceedingly imperative. Routinely planned breaks from work can be critical to helping you battle burnout in your entrepreneurial journey.

Sometimes you must go backward in order to move forward. Burnout is very real and doesn't always get triggered by something you are doing for the business. A phenomenon occurs when we have so many external obligations, obstacles, and opportunities. A fragmentation takes place within us and we eventually become disconnected from our authentic selves and disinterested in what's around us. This pattern of staying busy and hyper focused with no downtime became a part of who I was and how I shaped my experiences as an adult, mother, and entrepreneur. For example, shortly after birthing my fourth child, I opened a store in New York, launched *Raine Magazine*, and continued to run my fashion company—all at the same time. For me, successfully completing a task, project, or goal was always a big win.

I ran my life on tight schedules, high expectations, and the need to succeed. Failure meant more than letting me down, it meant letting my parents, family, and anyone else close to me down. Therefore, failure, giving up, or letting go was never an option. However, looking back, I realize now that I was on autopilot, going through the motions and checking off my to-do lists. As long as my objectives were accomplished successfully, I was happy. However, this was a false sense of happiness. What really made me happy was when I was living in the moment and experiencing the joy of learning something new.

Perhaps this was the reason why I loved designing so much. Each garment posed a new challenge, a new strategy for completion, a new purpose. Every time I created a new piece in my collection, met a new client, or had to produce a new show, I was always learning. The busier I became, the less time I could dedicate to learning, which resulted in the feeling of stagnation and boredom. My projects became less fun and more of a burden. This is when designing stopped being fun.

Shortly after my youngest turned one year old, I woke up with a desire that I couldn't shake. About 1:30 in the morning I sat up in my bed with this powerful need to get on my computer and look for a new house. Not in New York where we lived for the past seven years with our children, but across the country, in California. The thought shocked me because, prior to that moment, I never had any desire to leave New York. (Not to mention the fact that we had only been in our new house for three years.) My eldest was eight now and we were settling into a new routine with my parents who decided to move to New York to be closer to their grandchildren. So, why the sudden urge to look for homes so far away from everyone I loved, the city I obsessed over for so long, and the businesses I built? Looking back, I can now say that my inner soul was screaming for me to put a screeching halt to everything and subconsciously I thought that getting as far away from my current life was the answer. Deep down, I was burning out. All the things that once inspired me were now the very things slowly sucking the life out of me. It was time to make a change and my inner self decided to intervene.

It is important to pay attention to the signs of burnout. When you notice that you are heading in this direction, decide what you can put on pause for the moment. According to the Mayo Clinic, here are a few questions to ask yourself if you are experiencing burnout:

- Have you become cynical or critical at work?
- Do you drag yourself to work and have trouble getting started?
- Have you become irritable or impatient with co-workers, customers, or clients?
- Do you lack the energy to be consistently productive?
- Do you find it hard to concentrate?
- Do you lack satisfaction from your achievements?
- Do you feel disillusioned about your job?
- Are you using food, drugs, or alcohol to feel better or to simply not feel?
- Have your sleep habits changed?
- Are you troubled by unexplained headaches, stomach or bowel problems, or other physical complaints?

If you answered yes to any of the questions above, you may be in the midst of burning out. However, recognizing this as early as possible is very important because symptoms can be reversed, so don't despair. Fortunately, there are a lot of things you can do to recapture your energy and begin to feel positive and cheerful once more. To start, make an effort to set objectives for what must be completed and what can be paused to avoid getting tired. Get some rest when you are feeling worn out, and don't be afraid to ask for help when you need it. Taking care of yourself reestablishes prosperity and secures your well-being.

When we experience an extreme episode of depression during our entrepreneurial journey, we need to make it a priority to find ways to feel more energetic and reignite our entrepreneurial passions. For me, making a drastic move to add more blue and green (in other words, water and nature) into my life reignited my passion as an entrepreneur. My Jamaican roots, being an island girl, was calling loud and clear. That early morning search started in California but eventually led our family to Florida just two years later.

LONELINESS IS A STATE OF MIND

Entrepreneurial loneliness is a side effect of separating yourself from others as you develop your business. Only you can feel the relentless pull toward accomplishing the goals set out before you because you and only you can intimately understand your "why" and your purpose. Therefore, bringing your creation to life can bring with it feelings of loneliness and sadness. The good news is that these emotions can be calmed. Loneliness is a state of social disengagement, quietness, and extended episodes of isolation. As an entrepreneur, it is imperative to maintain an enthusiastic attitude by continuously seeking new connections and sustaining existing relationships to inspire you and keep you motivated. Additionally, create a routine where you regularly converse with loved ones. Calling, emailing, or writing family and friends are simple and effective ways to manage and conquer entrepreneurial loneliness.

EMBRACE BOREDOM WHEN IT COMES

If not addressed acutely, boredom can lead you on a downward spiral to the demise of your business. On the flip side, if recognized early enough, boredom can play a more positive role in your personal growth. Did you ever think that you could benefit from the simple task of letting your thoughts lead you wherever they want? This can only happen when the brain is in a resting state. Therefore, if properly addressed, boredom can be a useful signal for your psychological well-being. Daydreaming or staring off into space can be a significant rest for your mind and give you a short getaway from everyday life. Taking this type of break can be an important chance to revive, so go ahead and embrace boredom when it comes.

> "One must still have chaos in oneself to be able to give birth to a dancing star."
> —Friedrich Nietzsche

HOW TO STAY INSPIRED AS A CREATIVE ENTREPRENEUR

Entrepreneurship is a constant juggling act. If you are early on in your mission to become a creative entrepreneur, you may be struggling to make your dream attainable. If you have been on the road to entrepreneurship for quite a while, you have likely already dealt with several setbacks. Even when all is going well, inspiration can be fleeting. Before you know it, your business has overwhelmed your life, and the venture you once adored has become the very thing that is driving you crazy. Now what?

The answer is to take breaks, as many as you need in as many forms that are required. To keep your fire going, you need to step back and fan it from a distance. It's easy to get lost when you are constantly trudging through the forest, but if you take a moment to step outside the trees or even hover above them, you can easily gain a fresh perspective. Find ways to set limits around your time and use the free time you reserve for yourself to only do things that light you up or turn you on. It is your responsibility to keep your blaze burning.

The secret to remaining inspired as a creative entrepreneur is recollecting why you set out on your journey—often. Create a strategy from this day forward to implement methods needed to stay refreshed and excited. You must constantly recharge your batteries with the goal of returning more grounded after giving yourself "play" time. Remaining positive and true to your aspirations will enable you to successfully achieve your objectives.

YOUR FOURTEEN-DAY INSPIRATION PLAN

Each day for the next two weeks, review one item from the list below and create a plan to incorporate or update that part of your inspiration plan.

Day 1: Set individual objectives: When starting a business, most people create a plan that includes their objectives, goals, and beliefs, but most people also neglect to make their own personal plan which includes those same tenets. Record your personal objects, goals, and beliefs about yourself, and keep them handy so that you can peruse them whenever you need inspiration.

Day 2: Focus on your well-being: Stress is unavoidable yet figuring out how to adapt to it is urgent. Some people frequently neglect to take care of themselves physically. They often wait until they are sick or mentally fatigued before they start paying attention to their health. Physical well-being can have a very positive effect on your psychological well-being as well, so it is pivotal to your creative mind that you take good care of your health.

Day 3: Make a morning schedule: To ensure that you have a productive day, begin your day committed to that goal by creating a list of daily objectives. Make 75 percent of your objectives business-related and 25 percent individual. This will help you be less distracted by personal activities and keep you focused on your monetary or operational goals.

Day 4: Engage in leisure activities: You do not need to be solely focused on your work. Take time to explore different experiences that you enjoy. These healthy additions can help you discover activities that can actually stir your creative abilities. In your "play" time, you could watch stimulating or comedic movies, tune in to intriguing podcasts, or listen to inspirational music. These exercises can be performed at home while cooking dinner or driving.

Day 5: Set a challenge with your friends and family: The best type of inspiration you can get is from your loved ones. They can lift you up when you're feeling low, salute you when you accomplish your ideal achievements, and support you when you are in a slump. Sharing your day with loved ones can also lighten your load.

Day 6: Reward yourself: Give yourself personal motivators by rewarding yourself for a job well done. Regardless of whether they're big or small, your ongoing triumphs are achievements toward the overall success of your business. Compensating yourself is a powerful way to encourage you to continue to push through, no matter how hard the climb seems ahead of you.

Day 7: Get your sources of motivation ready: Nobody is pumped up 100 percent of the time, but with the right sources of motivation, you can get inspired instantly. Have your pre-selected content ready to tap into when you need help staying on track. You will be shocked by what a simple video or TED Talk can accomplish for your mental stimulation.

Day 8: Identify your greater inspiration: Build a business that influences the lives of those your business serves—a business that creates both opportunity and monetary security. Get clear on your main goal and the reasons that shape the moves you are making. If you are solving world problems, you need a great deal of steady inspiration to push through the difficult occasions. Identifying this greater inspiration will fuel you and all the individuals who work with you as well.

Day 9: Build a daily schedule: Figure out the general goal for your schedule, separating the highest priority tasks from the ones with the least priority. Setting up a strong routine will help you prosper as a creative entrepreneur by saving you time.

Day 10: Monitor the numbers: Monitor your achievements and record them so you can track where you are winning. Make a daily objective for yourself and assess if it is attainable or not. This will inspire you to stay on track with your goals and objectives.

Day 11: Create a positive workspace: Remaining engaged and forward-thinking is one of the greatest challenges that entrepreneurs will face. Create an extremely positive workplace by surrounding yourself with encouraging affirmations, uplifting imagery, and empowering elements. This may feel silly to do at first, but these small actions can yield big results.

Day 12: Revisit your "why": Whenever you feel overwhelmed or like you need an additional boost of inspiration, revisit the reason why you started your entrepreneurial journey in the first place. Maybe you were unhappy with your corporate job or had a strong desire to help others in your own unique way. When you keep your "why" at the forefront of your mind, you can jump-start renewed interest in entrepreneurial dreams. This reminder can help you through your tough days.

Day 13: Create balance: As an entrepreneur, you control your time and your schedule. This can be a good or bad thing. Self-motivation and determination often drive us to work well over forty, fifty, or sixty hours a week in our own businesses. This can lead to an imbalance of work and family life. As tempting as it is to keep working until the job, task, or to-do list is done, balance is more important. There are exceptional circumstances that may come up now and then, but by creating boundaries early on, this occurrence will happen less often than you think. Focus on being fully engaged with your friends, family, and even yourself when you are "off" the clock. Everyone will reap the benefits.

Day 14: Work out: When creating moments in your schedule to de-stress or reward yourself, try not to burn through the entirety of your breaks gazing at a screen. When you are disappointed about an outcome of a project or meeting or simply just feeling overworked, a little cardio or weightlifting session can do some amazing things. Exercise helps clear your head, calm your nerves, and can give you the feeling of control when you need it most.

W.O.W

We are all capable of burning brighter than the sun.

CONCLUSION

Even while writing this book, I was challenged with reexamining my "why." As an artist, I love to perform and entertain. As an individual, I like to retreat and enjoy my privacy. As a writer, I had to learn to be okay with being vulnerable as the stories shared are my personal triumphs and failures, my unique voyage and what I have learned along the way. As I conclude the book, I can only hope that you will find words that inspire you, empower you, and encourage you to go into the world and achieve whatever feat you put in front of you. This goal can solely be about entrepreneurship or not at all.

As I recalled my experiences and the many things I learned along the way, I took away a new meaning and purpose. I realized that although I set out to create a book that could help others more smoothly transition into entrepreneurship and more pleasantly evolve on the journey, I have also discovered that this book was just as much for me as for my readers. It was a journey of remembering where I started, taking time to appreciate the victories, reflect on the mistakes, and prepare for the greatness ahead. No matter where you start, you are always in the same place as I just described, in a place where we can remember, reflect, and prepare. During these times, we are reminded to slow down, be in the moment, take a look around to notice the tiniest flowers, or the fallen leaves from the trees, the children playing across the street, or the humming of the fan in the background. It is about recognizing our growth and deciding where we want to go from here.

These moments remind us that life is about choice, surprises, joys, and memories. As I share my words of wisdom within this book's pages, I too am continuing to learn from its very lessons. As I complete the chapters and conclude this journey of authorship, I recognize how much more I have learned about patience, persistence, belief, imagination, inspiration, motivation, and creation.

Every day, I am in awe of all that we can accomplish as creative beings. I admire our desire as entrepreneurs to solve the problems around us. I am humbled by the desire of so many to help the communities around them and I am propelled forward by the determination of those that follow, those that have not begun to embark on their dreams, those that are in the midst of a pivot, life change, or major altering of their current reality. I am encouraged by the moms and dads who choose this adventure of uncertainty. Having gone through it and still in it, I truly sympathize with the challenge of finding balance between career and family. My advice to you is to stay the course, forgive yourself often, and when you show up, no matter if it's for your children, your team, or your clients, be fully present—really and truly show up—in mind, body, and spirit.

Entrepreneurship truly is a game in which some win and some lose. It's up to you to decide which side of the court you will be on when the bell rings or the whistle is blown. Will you be holding the trophy or your head down in defeat? Additionally, I challenge you to be honest with yourself through this entire process, for that in and of itself is a victory. The point of this book isn't to convince you that entrepreneurship is the best thing ever invented or the answer to all of the world's problems. My mission with this book is to give you that extra pat on the back, that voice in the corner cheering you on, the whisper in the ear to help navigate you down this long but exciting road; and while you are on it, to enjoy every minute of it.

Now, for those that have been reading along from the beginning of this book, I promised to tell you what I finally decided on pursing, after receiving several admission letters into almost all of the fashion schools I applied for. I was left with a decision to either go on to receive my PhD in clinical psychology or instead enroll in fashion design school. If you read through this book carefully, by now you know what I eventually settled on.

I pivoted to study fashion design after completing my master's. After graduating from F.I.T., I spent about three years in corporate America. Following that, I pursued training in entrepreneurship and marketing before opening my own fashion design company. I later started consulting with creative entrepreneurs. I launched a magazine and opened a store. I then went in-house to launch a start-up into Macy's. I finally had to move and took the time to raise four children while building a media platform and continuing my consulting, including opening a showroom for new designers. Since then, I have written a book, screenplay, stage play, performed lived theater, launched an award-winning podcast, and booked a TedX Talk.

Currently, I am working on several fictional writing projects while stepping back into fashion design. Entrepreneurship is a beautiful journey of life, one that if appropriately traveled, can lead to boundless fulfillment. I am still on that journey; seeking more experiences in pursuit of unleashing my supernova. I am not there yet, but I know that I am getting there. Every step takes me closer to the point of divine fulfillment that I know is inside of me. I want to leave a legacy that lives on for the greater good long after I am gone. Feel free to get in touch with me through www.novalorraine.com at any point on your entrepreneurial journey, and I will be glad to share some words of wisdom to help you on your path.

I BELIEVE

I believe you can never stop learning or growing
as long as you are breathing.
I believe that everything in life prepares us
for the moment we are living at that time.
We have everything we need to survive any experience
thrust upon us
no matter when it comes.
It is up to us how we want to perceive that experience
and how it will affect us, good or bad.
—Nova Lorraine

BONUS TIPS

In case you missed any of the previous tips or just feel like getting more . . . check out the additional tips for boosting creativity and beating burnout below.

BOOST CREATIVITY

1. **Unplug**: Sometimes our best ideas come to us when we're not wracking our brains trying to come up with our best ideas. Instead, relax. Let your mind wander. You might get your next idea in the shower, shopping, driving, or exercising.

2. **Go for a walk**: Stanford research has indicated that walking improves creative thinking. In a follow-up study, the Harvard Business Review (HBR) found that people who take part in walking are more creative and engaged.

3. **Set the mood**: It has been drilled into us since school that complete silence is the best setting to work in. If this works for you, great! If not, try playing music to boost your mood and creativity.

4. **Ask for advice**: Sometimes you can be too close and invested in a project to see the problem. Why not ask a friend, family member, or anyone you trust to offer their unique perspective? Even if you don't use their advice, it may spark some new, creative thinking that will get you where you need to go.

5. **The kids are alright**: Children are so open-minded and innovative that they can more often than not find solutions to any problem they face. Ask your kids or children in your family how they would approach an issue, or even tap into your inner child and think, *what would my childhood self do*?

6. **Collaborate**: Discuss your work with peers and other experts. Just talking about it out loud may be enough to boost your creativity and spark some new ideas.

7. **Always have a pen and paper**: A 1938 study by Maclay, Guttmann, and Mayer-Gross found that the brain can be highly creative when you doodle. The busy, conscious side of the brain can be calmed down by doodling, which increases the opportunity for creative insight to be achieved. It'll also mean you're prepared the moment creativity strikes!

8. **Switch it up**: Psychologist Dr. Simone Ritter from Radboud University has found that changing simple routines, such as the way you make your usual sandwich, can help boost levels of creativity.

9. **Take risks**: When it comes to building your creative skills, you need to be willing to take risks in order to advance your abilities. While your efforts may not lead to success every time, you will still be boosting your creative talents and building skills that will serve you well in the future.

10. **Look for sources of inspiration**: Never expect creativity to just happen. Look for new sources of inspiration that will give you fresh ideas and motivate you to generate unique answers to questions. Read a book, visit a museum, listen to your favorite music, or engage in a lively debate with a friend.

11. **Meditate**: Stuck in a mental rut? When panic strikes, try meditating. It promotes divergent thinking, a state of mind in which we're able to generate new ideas.

12. **Be kind to yourself**: One of the most important ways to boost creativity is to have fun and not stress about the process! Remember, it's all about the journey, not the destination.

13. **Commit to it**: Set goals and make time for your creative pursuits.

14. **Reward yourself**: When pursuing something creative, we can often feel like we are indulging ourselves. Instead, reward yourself for your creativity. No one else will produce the same content/product as you.

15. **Build your confidence**: Insecurity in your abilities can suppress creativity, which is why it is important to build confidence. Make note of the progress you have made and commend your efforts.

16. **Overcome negativity**: Eliminate negative thoughts and self-criticisms that may impair your ability to develop strong creative skills.

17. **Fight your fear of failure**: The fear that you may make a mistake on your creative journey may halt your progress.

Whenever worries of failure enter your thoughts, remind yourself that failure is just part of the process and will shape you in a unique way.

18. **Brainstorm**: Brainstorming is a common technique in both academic and professional settings, but it can also be a powerful tool for developing your creativity. The goal is to generate as many ideas as possible in a relatively short span of time. Next, focus on clarifying and refining your ideas in order to arrive at the best possible choice.

19. **Six hats technique**: This is a technique in which a problem is approached from multiple perspectives. This produces more ideas than if you looked at a problem from just your perspective.[1]
    - **Red hat:** Look at the situation emotionally. What do your feelings tell you?
    - **White hat:** Look at the situation objectively. What are the facts?
    - **Yellow hat:** Use a positive perspective. Which elements of the solution will work?
    - **Black hat:** Use a negative perspective. Which elements of the solution won't work?
    - **Green hat:** Think creatively. What are some alternative ideas?
    - **Blue hat:** Think broadly. What is the best overall solution?

20. **Snowball technique**: This is the idea that you start with a core idea and build on it, like a snowball rolling down a snow-covered slope. [2]

---

1 Edward de Bono, Edward (1985). Six Thinking Hats: An Essential Approach to Business Management. Little, Brown, & Company.

2 Sergey Markov, Snowballing technique, Genius Revive.com (2018) https://geniusrevive.com/en/snowballing-technique/.

- One slip of paper is used per idea generated or possible solution offered.
- A meeting is set up of up to five people. The slips of paper are viewed and then grouped "like with like."
- Duplicates can be created if the idea is relevant to more than one group.
- Patterns and relationships in the groups are observed.

21. **Remove expectations**: Don't pressure yourself with high expectations, you'll be more creative then.

22. **Read, read, read!**: Reading is one of the best ways to stimulate the mind, while also relaxing it. Reading opens the mind to new ways of thinking while increasing creativity.

23. **Do something new**: Give your creativity a huge boost by doing something you've never done before. It may give you a new perspective that can be applied to your work.

24. **Play chess:** It may not sound like the most creative activity but a study in Alabama concluded that chess improved test scores and excitement about coming to school, more so in the lower grades.[3] Even teachers who taught chess reported being more excited about their jobs. Boost your creativity by learning how to play chess.

25. **Daydream:** Learn to use your imagination. You must see it in your mind before it becomes a reality. Become a master of visualization.

3 George Chitiyo Ph.D., Lisa Zagumny, Ph.D., Ashley B. Akenson, Ph.D., Michael Littrell, Krista Davis, Kevin Besnoy, Ph.D., "Teaching with Chess: Exploring the Relationship between Chess and Student Learning Outcomes," ACIS Years 1-3 Report 2018, (2019).

BEAT BURNOUT

1. **Reset your standards (temporarily)**: As creatives, we are renowned for setting high standards for our work. Achieving creative perfection is difficult enough on its own, but coupled with looming deadlines, professional peer pressure, and other strains, it's simply impossible to always produce perfect creative work. So, step back, recharge, and accept that the standard of work you produce will have to be a little lower than usual, which is better than not being able to produce anything at all.

2. **Think about projects that boosted your creativity (and ones that didn't)**: This exercise should help you to identify the common factors that help your creativity flourish, as well as the factors that dampen it. Perhaps you are most creative in the context of a pressing deadline, or maybe these deadlines are more likely to lead you toward creative block.

3. **Be creative through other activities**: Experiencing creative burnout doesn't mean that your creative abilities have completely deserted you, although it can certainly feel that way. If you feel unable to draw, take photos, or create design work, it just means your brain needs to take a break from these activities for a while.

4. **When and where are you most creative?**: Most creatives have a designated space for work activities, whether it's a home office, studio, or co-working space. While this is good practice for establishing a professional routine, it's also possible that this space is contributing to feelings of burnout. If you're suffering from burnout symptoms, try to track how you feel, as well as how productive and creative you are

throughout the day. Map these to the environments you're in and the times when these fluctuations occur.

5. **Start small**: One of the things that can make exhausted creatives feel worse and in fact worsen the problem of burnout is attempting to tackle a big project. Even if you manage to complete a large task it's very unlikely that it will be of high quality when you're struggling with burnout. You need to build up slowly to large tasks again by attempting small, achievable tasks instead. Begin with a job that has a creative element but doesn't feel overwhelming.

6. **Allow yourself to relax**: Watch that movie. Binge that show. Play that album on repeat. It may not feel like you're doing anything productive because our culture encourages nonstop work. But when you take in other media, you can become inspired to boost your creativity and beat burnout.

7. **Listen to your body first**: Make sure you're eating, sleeping, and exercising enough. Once you have a strong physical framework in place, you can more easily carve out time and energy in your daily life to conquer your creative goals.

8. **Talk to someone who gets it**: Your friends and family may be supportive, but sometimes they don't fully understand the struggle of losing drive in your work. By engaging your peers, you can vent to someone who understands and has probably been in the same position as you.

9. **Break ties**: Although it may sound harsh, being around people who create a negative workspace or put you in a pessimistic mindset are not good for your work in the first place. They definitely aren't good when you're already burnt

out. Set boundaries and surround yourself with people who encourage and support you, even when you're struggling with creativity.

10. **Get organized**: Doesn't sound very creative, I know. But much of the stress we experience daily is from being disorderly and not knowing what to do next. Organize what you have to, then you can focus on the creative process.

11. **Pick a goal**: Decide on one goal or focus each time you work. This could be an introductory paragraph or a whole chapter; a rough sketch or a detailed illustration; a single screen design or an entire user flow. You should be going for depth, not breadth, here, and should be careful not to bite off more than you can chew. Focus your idea, and follow-through will become more manageable.

12. **Don't slip back into burnout habits**: Thankfully, burnout is temporary. Once you've rediscovered your creative spark and started working at full capacity once again, it can be easy to slip into old habits. However, if some of those habits were contributing to creative fatigue, it's likely that burnout will strike again.

13. **Reach out**: Opening up won't make you a burden to others. In fact, most friends and loved ones will be flattered that you trust them enough to confide in them, and it will only strengthen your friendship. Talking about your burnout will relieve some of the pressure it can cause.

14. **Move on**: A lot of the time, burnout and blocks come from a specific project. So, move on to something else and you'll be flowing in no time.

15. **Due date**: Give yourself a deadline. This may motivate you to get the project done—racing against the clock will give you a much-needed creative boost.

16. **Be a sponge**: Observe creative processes of other people and see if you can apply their techniques to your work.

17. **Go big**: Think of the wildest, biggest idea without worrying about cost or practicality, then work back until it becomes feasible. Once you've thought of crazy ideas, what you can achieve seems more doable.

18. **Use your walls**: Put your ideas on the wall, this way you can visualize and tweak with ease. Don't keep it all in your head; make some room in your brain.

19. **Practice "easy stuff"**: Sometimes the most difficult part of the creative process is beginning. When you are burned out from overworking and overextending yourself on projects, returning to the fundamentals of your craft can often inspire creativity. This can reintroduce you to the joy of your creative process and create a space where you can relax.

20. **Break things into smaller pieces**: What are the smallest meaningful pieces to work with? Work on a page. Can't do a page? Work on a paragraph. Get down to the smallest bit you feel you can manage but do it.

21. **Look at the worst pieces of work you know of**: The worst writing. The worst painting. The worst web design. The worst whatever. Does it annoy you? Do you feel inspired to change it or redirect it?

22. **Change your work environment**: What do you do at work when you feel stuck? Are there things you can do to your cube or office to help you deal with those times? You spend eight hours a day in that space, it's worth taking a couple of hours to improve it by even 5 or 10 percent.

23. **Career and lifestyle**: How long have you been doing what you're doing? Do you expect to do it forever? Perhaps you need bigger changes in your life. A new city, a new company, or a new hobby might be the only way to move your life forward.

24. **Set priorities**: There are three ways you can label what needs to be done to help you better prioritize your tasks:
    1. Urgent: These items have to be done by the end of the day.
    2. Important: These items have a later due date but might require a little more focus.
    3. Can wait: Let's face it—some things can wait.

25. **Pay attention to your thoughts**: If you find yourself feeling more sensitive to feedback or more drained at the end of the day, it might be time to take a break.

INDEX

D

E

F

G

ABOUT THE AUTHOR

Without inspiration, there is no creativity;
without creativity, there is no life.

~

Nova Lorraine has spent twenty years in the creative industry in roles such as founder, fashion designer, consultant, editor, publisher, and writer. She intimately understands the growing pains of entrepreneurship and the constant challenge of staying inspired while growing a business. Over a decade ago, she founded *Raine*, a magazine dedicated to the lifestyle of the creative entrepreneur. In her writings, she shares her personal experiences along with tips gained from her interviews with many successful individuals such as Mark Cuban, Daymond John, Nikki Hilton, Julian Marley, Priyanka Chopra, and Kendall Jenner, to name a few. Nova is now a resident of Pennsylvania. She travels across the country while staying involved in the lives of her four very active, creative, and athletic children.

LIMITLESS

Why? You ask.
Why Not? I answer.
You are the ruler of worlds
A thunderous force of nature
Never underestimate your power
It lies dormant inside of you like a sleepy caterpillar
Just waiting for the right moment to break free as a newly born butterfly
Seeking to taste the beauty of the open air and sky
Feeling no boundaries
Just the limitless capacity of the wind
Rise my star
Your rays thaw glaciers
Your beauty blinds the sun
It is your untapped passion that can erupt volcanoes and move oceans
It is your duty to fill all the buckets of your desire.
Why? I ask.
Why Not? You answer.

—Nova Lorraine